W9-BWM-477

Rita Ferrone

■

On the Rite
of Election

Sac (RCIA)

4008

Fer

Liturgy Training Publications
in cooperation with

The North American Forum on the Catechumenate

ST. MARY'S RELIGIOUS ED. OFFICE
7401 40TH AVENUE
KENOSHA, WISCONSIN 53142

Acknowledgments

The Forum Essay series is a cooperative effort of The North American Forum on the Catechumenate and Liturgy Training Publications. The purpose of this series is to provide a forum for exploring issues emerging from the implementation of the order of Christian initiation and from the renewal of the practice of reconciliation in the Roman Catholic Church.

Other titles in the series:

The Role of the Assembly in Christian Initiation
Catherine Vincie

Eucharist as Sacrament of Initiation
Nathan D. Mitchell

Preaching and Christian Initiation
J. Michael Joncas (Winter 1995)

Forum Essays was designed by Mary Bowers and typeset in Futura and Bembo style by Jim Mellody-Pizzato. The cover photograph is by Vicky Grayland. Photo courtesy of Pioneer Press. Editorial assistance was provided by Deborah Bogaert and Theresa Pincich. Editors for the series are Victoria M. Tufano (Liturgy Training Publications) and Thomas H. Morris (The North American Forum on the Catechumenate).

Library of Congress Cataloging-in Publications Data

Ferrone, Rita.
On the Rite of election/Rita Ferrone.
p. cm.—(Forum essays; no. 3)
Includes bibliographical references.
ISBN 1-56854-025-6 (pbk.): $6.00
1. Catholic Church. Rite of election. 2. Initiation rites—Religious aspects—Catholic Church. 3. Catechumens—Recruiting—United States. 4. Catholic Church—United States—Membership. I. Title. II. Series.
BX2045.I55F47 1994
264'.020813—dc20   94-10735
                                                                    CIP

CONTENTS

■

Introduction

The starting place for my investigations is both the most obvious one and the one most taken for granted—namely, the fact that we have on our hands a rite called "election." Why *election?* That the early church referred to those chosen for baptism at Easter as *electi,* while significant, is surely not reason enough. They were also called *competentes* and *illuminandi,* yet the rite is not named the "Rite of Competence" or the "Rite of Illumination." Nor does it seem sufficient to suggest that election refers solely to the concrete action of the church in choosing these catechumens to receive the initiation sacraments, and that it is therefore simply named for the choosing we undertake together. While the rite makes clear that the church acts in the transition called election, it makes it equally clear that the event is not solely about what we do among ourselves. The rite explicitly rejects such an interpretation when it claims the choosing as God's.[1]

1

By taking pains to accord priority to God's action, the rite asserts its fundamentally theological orientation. The action of the church follows upon the action of God. Election by the church is about divine election. I am convinced that if we miss this basic theological orientation, we have missed the central point of the rite, however well we may have grasped its details. So our question, still unanswered, is sharpened a bit: Why is God's election a mystery of such pivotal importance to initiation that we are summoned to remember it at this critical juncture in the catechumenate process?

And it is a critical juncture. In the so-called provisional text of the *Rite of Christian Initiation of Adults,* issued in English in 1974, election was called "the turning point of the whole catechumenate."[2] The most obvious reason for considering election the turning point is, of course, that the discernment that precedes the Rite of Election makes this juncture the most decisive one. This phrase also suggests, however, that the catechumenate is like a dramatic action that has been long in building and is now reaching its denouement. We have all known plays, movies and novels that do this. Slowly, gradually, the characters are introduced; their virtues, weaknesses, conflicts and passions are revealed; and then, like a thunderclap before the downpour, something "goes off," explodes or snaps into place. Suddenly the plot accelerates as events start galloping at a furious pace toward their resolution.

Election is such a turning point. The rite presumes a long catechumenate—a slow, patient, gradual process taking months and even years—that follows a precatechumenate that is also substantial. Once election is celebrated, a vigorous, even strenuous, Lent follows, with fasting and prayer and scrutinies and presentations. All this leads us to a breathtaking Easter Vigil—the climax of all the ritual activity preceding it. And the Vigil is followed by a generous mystagogy. To say that election is a turning point is not to minimize the Easter Vigil, which is the climax of the whole process, but is to claim that election is the turning point that leads to that climax.

This brings us back to our question: Why is this precipitating event named *election?* To answer that question, we must look at what election means. This discussion, which I will take up in chapter three, is at the heart of the matter and will provide support for all the subsequent points I wish to raise about the practical aspects of the rite itself.

If we know what to look for, we readily see the theology of election reflected in the modern rite. We see references to election in the prayers and other symbolic texts of the rite and see allusions to it in the readings for the First Sunday of Lent. These readings, about primordial disaster, sin and temptation, can seem like strange visitors in a liturgy that has been conceived as a kind of great festival of affirmation. But they are anything but incongruous to the Christian tradition concerning election. The readings do not make a systematic presentation of election, but they call it to mind in evocative and quite specific ways.

At the same time, we do well to remember that the Rite of Election is rooted in the very basic task of collecting the names of those who are ready to be baptized at the Easter Vigil. The rite has business to transact. That business has a profound meaning, but business it remains, and if we lose touch with this aspect of what the rite is up to, we go astray. The Rite of Election loses its grounding if this very concrete matter does not get the attention it deserves or is rendered superfluous by the Rite of Sending.[3]

I begin part I with a consideration of some of the ancient precedents for the Rite of Election because I believe that the historical sources provide important clues to a correct understanding of the modern rite. Historical material appears in other sections as well, to help us take the long view while grappling with present-day issues. Chapter two presents my interpretation of the *editio typica* and reviews the adaptations of the Rite of Election contained in the 1988 English translation approved for use in the United

States. The chapter concludes with a report on recent pastoral and liturgical developments concerning this rite in the United States.

Over the past several years we have witnessed the growth and increasing complication of liturgical matters relating to the Rite of Election. In the 1988 edition of the *Rite of Christian Initiation of Adults* approved for use in the dioceses of the United States, seven rites are available to mark this juncture in the catechumenate.[4] Each of these rites is different; some are optional, some required; certain of them entail certain others. The number of dioceses holding celebrations has grown, the number of diocesan celebrations within dioceses has increased, and attendance at them has flourished. Local adaptations and innovations have developed, various understandings and assumptions about the nature and purpose of these rites have taken shape. Some of these developments have raised new questions about the meaning of the rite.

I have chosen four particular phenomena for special critical attention in part II, which comprises chapters four through seven. In chapter four, I will discuss the problems associated with an overemphasis on the role of episcopal presidency at the rite. In chapter five, I will discuss the problems of conceiving the Rite of Election as a welcome to the diocesan church. In chapter six, I will discuss difficulties that have come up in connection with the book of the elect. And in chapter seven, I will discuss some catechetical issues relating to the preparation of catechumens and candidates for the rite.

The rite itself and the traditions concerning election, I believe, offer us guidance in all these areas. Along with illustrating what I see as the "pathologies" that have emerged in practice, I also hope to point out some directions that are faithful to the spirit of the rite. There is more than one way to celebrate this rite, and any good examples I offer are intended to illustrate points, not to substitute for the work of local planning. I am interested primarily in the

4

criteria we use to determine the appropriateness of what we do, not in creating a single mold or ideal final product.

The aforementioned discussions do not, of course, exhaust the many issues that could and should be taken up in relation to the Rite of Election. For example, a much longer discussion of the implications of the combined rite for unbaptized and baptized candidates really should be taken up in the context of a thorough consideration of principles relating to the adaptation of rites for the baptized. A thorough treatment of these complex questions is quite beyond the scope of this work. Second, the limitations of both my own experience and the existing literature with regard to celebrating the Rite of Election with children of catechetical age have likewise made it impossible for me to do more than touch on this important area. Last of all, I am acutely aware that the multiethnic dimensions of diocesan celebrations like the Rite of Election are important, complex, extremely varied and need much more attention than I could give them here. My hope is that the topics I have been prepared to discuss may be of some help to others in sorting through certain aspects of these questions.

For the past ten years or so, I have been a very engaged observer of the Rite of Election. During this time I have seen the rite celebrated in parish churches and cathedrals, with small groups and large, on the First Sunday of Lent and at other times. I have planned diocesan rites in two dioceses, in cooperation with many capable and insightful colleagues, and had my experience enlarged considerably by many conversations with people across the country (in regional gatherings and particularly in institutes sponsored by The North American Forum on the Catechumenate) who have told me about what they do and what it means to them. The Rite of Election seems to bring out the best and the worst (and quite a lot in between) in the church that celebrates it.

Part of my project during the past ten years as an interested, critical observer has been to test my intuitions about the Rite of Election against historical data about the rite, against the material in the modern ritual book, against the theological and scriptural sources, and against my understanding of the framework of Christian initiation as a whole. After careful consideration, some of these intuitions have landed on the scrap heap. Those that proved true, and seemed to me useful, are included here.

Because our experience of the catechumenate is still so young, what we do at this stage, and what we think we are doing, can have great consequences for the future of this rite. By subjecting some recent developments to thoughtful criticism, we plan for that future. I hope the reader will understand that, on my part, this criticism does not reflect a dismissive attitude toward the zealous and earnest efforts of so many to celebrate this liturgy well and meaningfully, nor does it discount the religious value of the rites for those who experience them. No one knows better than I how much labor of love goes into preparing these celebrations or how high feelings run concerning them. My last intention is to disparage any of this. But our concern must always be about how we can secure a better future, lest our present efforts become the limit of our vision.

In the dialectical process of coming to understand better the Rite of Election, I have become more and more aware of the church's need to develop adequate critical standards for judging liturgical adaptations. This process begins not with the adaptation but with the rite itself. What "sense" do we find in the rite itself, and how do we go about finding it? It is only after we have addressed these questions that we can go on to ask: When do we feel called or compelled to adapt a rite, and what makes for a good adaptation? In a broad sense this is what this monograph is about, as much as it is about election itself. As such, it remains a very open-ended discussion.

I am grateful for all the support and help I received in the course of producing this work. Particular thanks are due Father Robert Duggan for his helpful suggestions throughout and for sharing his library; to Father Aidan Kavanagh, OSB, for his encouraging comments on the manuscript; to the International Commission on English in the Liturgy (ICEL) for providing access to research materials; and most of all to my husband, Dr. Philip Swoboda, who was an invaluable critical reader and whose faith in this project and its author made this monograph possible.

Chapter 1

The Historical Roots of the Rite

■

Many who would study the modern rites of initiation assume that reforms of the liturgy have to do with improving on the past, not with rediscovering and being inspired by it. When we look at a liturgical reform we ask how well it reflects where we are today, not what the historical sources reflected in it might have to teach us. As one of my incautious students expressed it, history is "dull and boring." Or as an undergraduate once said to his history professor, a friend of mine: "What are you so excited about, Mr. Ellis? It's history. It's over."

Yet it is impossible to perceive correctly the intentions and characteristic shape of our present-day Rite of Election, or indeed any of the rites of initiation of adults, without knowing something about the historical sources from which these rites are derived. Not every pastoral leader is, or needs to be, a historian of the rites; but to interpret the rites intelligently, and thus to have the tools to

9

lead the church wisely, one must know something about the history of the rites.

The *coetus,* or committee, that drafted the rites for the adult catechumenate after the Second Vatican Council did so with a conscious effort to invent as little as possible.[1] What they were commissioned to do was not to create but to restore the catechumenate.[2] Thus the project of remaining faithful to historical sources continually informed the decisions that were made.

Knowing the history can help make sense of the present Rite of Election. A case in point, albeit a minor one, is the name of the rite. Why is it the "Rite of Election *or* Enrollment of Names"? Couldn't they make up their minds what to call it? Does it matter if it is one or the other? Isn't it both? Does this reflect a theological ambivalence? One might argue that it would be more pastorally effective to have one name for a rite, but the reason for the two has nothing to do with the questions raised above. There is more than one name because the ritual was known in some places as election and in others as enrollment of names. Two alternative traditions were collected into one. Rather than reject one name, the modern rite keeps both. Similarly, the *praenotanda* make careful note of the fact that "the elect" themselves were called by various names, and list the Latin ones.[3] Why bother? Because the various traditions known through the historical sources show that various names were used. They are therefore legitimate, traditional options to preserve in the church today.

These are minor examples of a major concern: that the rites, their language, their structure and their symbolic texts should be based on what was done in the early centuries of the church's life, when the catechumenate flourished. This concern arises not out of mindless antiquarianism[4] but out of concern for keeping faith with the church's tradition. This concern is accompanied by the studied conviction that what the church actually did in those times vigorously reflected the gospel and promoted apostolic faith. The restored practices were intended to reflect the best of the church's long tradition of initiation.

As with all ancient precedents for modern liturgical rites, we do not know everything we might like to about the early history of the Rite of Election. But we do know a number of particular things about this rite. While its roots go back to a much earlier period—perhaps even to initiatory patterns found in the New Testament[5]—most of the sources that describe the characteristic features of the Rite of Election in any detail date from the fourth century. From these texts the following general profile emerges, which includes elements that are found in some earlier sources as well.

Election marked a transition in the catechumenate, from one period into another which immediately preceded baptism.[6] This period of final preparation for baptism coincided with Lent.[7] To make the transition into this period of proximate preparation for baptism, the catechumens had their *bona fides* for being "chosen" or "elected" established in this rite by the testimony of godparents and possibly others. This testimony was heard and accepted by the church, presided over by the bishop.[8] In this rite of election or enrollment, the catechumens also "gave in their names."[9] As a result of having participated in such a rite, the catechumens were called *electi* (the elect) or *competentes* (petitioners) in Latin-speaking churches; *photizomenoi* (those who are being enlightened) or *baptizomenoi* (those who are being baptized) in Greek-speaking churches; and, uniquely in Jerusalem, *fideles* (the faithful).[10] The new title indicated that a new status was conferred on the catechumen as the result of participating in this rite. Their election was followed by a more concentrated preparation for the sacraments of initiation, including scrutinies and catechesis on the gospel.

In order to draw out some specific observations from the foregoing generalizations, we will look briefly at two important sources. The first of these is the *Apostolic Tradition* of Hippolytus. This document is a church order; it gives instructions about how to carry out a variety of functions in the life of the church, such as initiation, ordination, fasting and the eucharist. This particular order claims to describe practices that go back to the church of the apostles, but this is almost certainly not the case. Written about 215 CE, it describes Roman liturgical practice for a period of perhaps 50 years previous to that time. During this period it was a crime to profess Christianity in the Roman Empire, and many Christians suffered persecution and martyrdom as a consequence of holding to their faith. Hippolytus himself was exiled to Sardinia at the end of his life and, like many other Christians at the time, died a martyr's death.[11]

Although the *Apostolic Tradition* was reconstructed from various sources and is therefore a complicated document about which scholars continue to argue, it is generally thought to contain reliable information about practices of the church in Rome. This document is thought to be ancestral to other church orders, such as the *Apostolic Constitutions* (375–400, Syria), the *Canons of Hippolytus* (335, Egypt) and the *Testamentum Domini* (fourth or fifth century, possibly in Asia Minor). The *Apostolic Tradition* is the earliest liturgical source that describes the catechumenate in any detail, and each bit of material in it gives us important clues to the early practices of the church. It does not contain all the material relevant to the Rite of Election, mentioned earlier, but only a brief instruction about the transition that election marks. What it does tell us, however, is significant for understanding the roots of the modern rite.

Second, we will look at *Egeria's Travels*, which provides a complete description of what a Rite of Election looked like in Jerusalem in the late fourth century. This is a source very different from the *Apostolic Tradition;* it is a collection of letters written by the Spanish nun Egeria to her sisters at home, describing her pilgrimage to Jerusalem. Egeria is a pious and enthusiastic pilgrim, eager to relate her experiences and all the things she observed in the course of her journey. Her account gives us detail and color and some sense of her response to what she saw. She also is considered to be a quite faithful reporter of facts. Her account gives us the clearest picture of what a Rite of Election was like in the late fourth century.

What Egeria saw in Jerusalem in about the year 400 reflects the changed situation of the catechumenate and the church after the peace of Constantine. Unlike Hippolytus, for whom the catechumenate period prior to election appears clearly to be a time of rigorous Christian formation, Egeria wrote at a time when the catechumenate period was in decline. The Christian formation given in the initial stage of the catechumenate was, in Egeria's day, spread out over many years and appeared to have lost much of its original rigor. Many scholars believe that the decline of the early part of the catechumenate caused more attention than ever to be given to the lenten preparation of catechumens for baptism. And it is true that Egeria describes an impressive, fully developed Rite of Election, whereas Hippolytus merely hints at the existence of a rite at that point. The rite she describes is celebrated at the beginning of Lent, whereas in earlier centuries the seasons of the liturgical year had not yet developed. And the enrollment of names, though highly symbolic, seems also to have served the church's need for greater organization as larger numbers of catechumens petitioned for baptism after Constantine made it legal for Christians to profess their faith. Both in their contrasts and in their continuities, these two sources can help us understand the origins of the modern Rite of Election.

Hippolytus of Rome

The *Apostolic Tradition* of St. Hippolytus of Rome tells of the choosing and setting apart of candidates for baptism after they have gone through a catechumenate lasting three years. It gives an instruction on how they are to be chosen and on what is to happen to them after they are elected.

In the *Apostolic Tradition* (AT), the entrance into the catechumenate and the election each include an examination. In the first instance, the candidates' initial dispositions upon coming to the catechumenate are questioned: "Those who bring them shall bear witness for them whether they are able to hear" (AT XVI.2),[12] and persons of various professions and statuses thought to be inimical to Christianity are screened out.

In the second instance, when they are to be chosen for baptism, the catechumens' evidence of piety and works of Christian charity during the catechumenate are weighed and considered. The criteria for passing from one stage to the other are that they have "lived piously while catechumens . . . honored the widows . . . visited the sick . . . fulfilled every good work" (AT XX.1). This rule of discernment is spiritual and moral, basic and not unduly subtle. The ones who brought them (their sponsors) could be expected to bear witness to these things.

There is no mention of the bishop having a role in the election itself. He only appears as baptism draws nearer. But the sponsors play a decisive role: "And when those who brought them bear witness to each, 'He has,' let them hear the gospel" (AT XX.1).[13] Once the sponsors have given their testimony about the catechumens, their status changes. They can "hear the gospel," hands are laid on them daily, and they are exorcised daily; as baptism draws nearer, the bishop himself performs the exorcism (AT XX.2–3). There is no specific mention of an enrollment of names, though by "choosing" and "setting aside," one obviously identifies certain catechumens.

Thus the *Apostolic Tradition* establishes that there was a transition in the catechumenate at this point, when certain of the catechumens were "chosen" for baptism. It also establishes that from the earliest history of the catechumenate, discernment by the church was thought to be necessary for this transition to take place. Hippolytus's rule for discernment stresses the Christian way of life. The *Apostolic Tradition* assures us that the witness of the godparents was important to the church from the earliest times. And, last of all, it shows that a time of more intense activity followed for the chosen after this decision was made in their favor.

Egeria's Account of Election in Jerusalem

Later sources have more to say about what a liturgy of election included. As was mentioned earlier, the one detailed description we have of the way enrollment for baptism was done comes from the Spanish nun Egeria, writing of her pilgrimage to the Holy Land in about the year 400. She says that the names of those seeking baptism had to be given to a presbyter before the beginning of their eight-week Lent. This determined who went before the bishop in the rite once Lent began.

Then, "at the start of the eight weeks" (E 45.2),[14] which was the extent of Lent in Jerusalem at that time, the catechumens who had given their names came before the bishop himself, who was seated in the midst of the great church. His presbyters were seated on each side of him, and all the clergy were standing. The scene was one of the whole governing board of the church assembled, with the bishop presiding. Leonel Mitchell suggests that they made a great semicircle, which the elect completed when they were enrolled, thus forming one great circle.[15]

They came forward to the bishop one by one, each with a godparent: "men coming with their fathers, and women with their mothers" (E 45.2). The questions that the bishop posed concerned the catechumens' way of life. He asked about conduct; for example, sobriety, obedience to parents, deceitfulness, and "all the serious human vices" (E 45.3). **15**

Some may have been rejected on the basis of this examination and told to amend their lives and come back later. On the other hand, if this inquiry into the character of the catechumen was successful and the bishop "proved him in the presence of witnesses to be blameless in all these matters" (E 45.4),[16] his name was then inscribed.

Whether the names were written in a book, on a scroll, or what, we do not know. But the distinction is not important. We know from the catechetical instructions of Theodore, bishop of Mopsuestia from 392 to 428, that his diocese had a "church book" for this purpose.[17] St. John Chrysostom, theologian and bishop, writing in Antioch at the end of the fourth century (388–390), also makes reference to such a book when he addresses the candidates as those "who have deserved to be enrolled in this heavenly book."[18]

Egeria notes that the names of the *competentes* are inscribed by the bishop's own hand (E 45.4), suggesting that she would have expected someone else to perform this chore— not the candidates themselves, since presumably few of them could read or write, but some scribal assistant. What she witnessed appears to be unique in this respect: No source for any other church records that the bishop wrote the names himself.[19]

Whatever the earlier preparation of the catechumens may have been at this period, it is clear from Egeria's account that the enrollment for baptism stepped up the pace of activity for the candidates considerably and brought the initiation process into greater public view. At the beginning of Lent, with the enrollment for baptism, the activities of those being initiated became more obviously central to the public life of the assembled community. Exorcisms, hand-layings and three hours of catechesis daily were to follow this event (E 46.1–4). The faithful were welcome at the catecheses given by the bishop—both before and after Easter—and they came in numbers. In fact, these sessions were greeted so enthusiastically at times that "the voices of those who applaud are so loud that they can be heard outside the church" (E 47.2).[20]

Egeria's Account and the Modern Rite of Election

As we set about making connections between the ancient rite and its modern counterpart, we must admit that what Egeria observed of the election of catechumens in Jerusalem would create severe problems for the modern church if adopted literally in any of its central features. The drama of actually deciding on the spot, publicly, who goes forward and who has to go home and try again next year is, to put it mildly, a little too wrenching for the modern psyche. The notion of putting forward an individual case for each candidate in modern dioceses that may have hundreds of adults seeking baptism is just impossible to realize. Even the idea of having the bishop inscribe each name would be impossible in any but the smallest of dioceses. And the sight of the bishop enthroned, flanked by seated presbyters and rows of standing clergy would intimidate any but the most stouthearted.

Nevertheless, in our modern Rite of Election the basic outline of judgment by the church under the leadership of the bishop, based on the testimony of witnesses, and then the enrollment of names, remains identical with this ancient model. Discernment—that critical component without which the rite is considered a sham, "mere formality"[21]— is, in the final analysis, a method of the church coming to a good decision about each candidate. The bishop as head of the local church presides over this judgment and is responsible for it in fact. That this discernment goes on outside of and prior to this ritual does not diminish its centrality to what happens in the rite. The godparents' ministry, then as now, is very important for this transition and for the period following election as well.

Last of all, the solemn enrollment of names forms as essential a component of the modern rite as it did in Egeria's account of enrollment in 400. The modern rite, presuming a higher literacy rate, offers as a first option that the elect write their names themselves. As a second option, the person who presented the catechumens, or a catechist, may write the names as the catechumens themselves call them out. Third, a list written beforehand may be presented if there are too many names to write on the spot.[22] Last of all, in a decision that corresponds to other ancient sources (as, for example, Theodore of Mopsuestia),[23] the *praenotanda* of the modern rite allow the godparents to write their names alongside those of the elect.[24] In all events, the inscription of names stands as a gesture of great importance in the modern rite, just as it did in Egeria's account of the liturgy of election in Jerusalem.

The modern order of Christian initiation of adults attempts to incorporate the virtues of a rigorous catechumenate period, such as Hippolytus knew, with a strong celebration of election and Lent, such as Egeria observed in Jerusalem almost two centuries later. In both cases, the church's election of catechumens to celebrate the sacraments was a turning point in the catechumenate—a moment of judgment. In later historical sources, such as *Egeria's Travels,* we see a well-developed, highly symbolic rite to accomplish this turning point—a rite that includes a solemn testimony by godparents and an inscription of the names of the elect.

Chapter 2

The Present Shape of the Rite

■

The term *editio typica* refers to the Latin text of a rite published by the Vatican. The *editio typica* of any rite of the Roman Catholic Church is the basis of all adaptations and extensions that episcopal conferences and local churches make.

The Norms of the *Editio Typica:* Some Comments

The Rite of Election as it is prescribed in the *editio typica* is quite simple and direct. Even more than the Rite of Acceptance into the Order of Catechumens, the Rite of Election is restrained in its texts and economical in its gestures. The *editio typica* describes a Rite of Election for adult catechumens presided over by the bishop. It normally takes place during the Mass of the First Sunday of Lent,

19

after a careful discernment of the readiness of the catechumens has been carried out. The rite begins after the homily and consists of the presentation of the catechumens, the questioning of their godparents, the affirmation by the catechumens, the enrollment of their names, the election, an instruction to the godparents, a gesture by the godparents of accepting the elect into their care, the intercessions for the elect, a prayer for the elect accompanied by extension of hands by the presider, and a dismissal.

The best way to conceive of what is going on in the rite is to see it as two main actions of comparable weight, in balance with one another, the second of which follows from the first and completes it: the testimony of the godparents and the enrollment of names.

Testimony of the Godparents   The first action, around which several events cluster, is the testimony of the godparents. Although such testimony was also taken in the ancient rite, the actual dialogue formulated for the testimony in the rite is not of ancient provenance; it is modern, based on pastoral experience with the catechumenate in France.[1] The names of the catechumens are called, and they come forward in order to have their progress in the Christian life attested to by their godparents. Of all the elements in the first part of the Rite of Election, the testimony of the godparents is the one with the deepest roots in the tradition, as we have seen. It is tremendously important as a statement of God's action in their lives and is the basis of the transition from the catechumenate period to the lenten period of purification and enlightenment. It is also the vital connecting link of the rite with the process of conversion that takes place through catechesis, community life, and so on.

The testimony determines the import of the presentation that came before it. The testimony, carried out in the presence of the bishop and of the assembled local church, makes this presentation different from something that might happen in a Rite of Acceptance or Welcome. True, the calling of names, the coming forward, the act of "putting one's self there," has a weight of symbolic significance and in a way resembles what is done at the Rite of Acceptance. But "putting one's self there" happens at every rite of the catechumenate. It is a constant, and it is therefore the variations in meaning that attach to it that are significant. The "here am I" of the candidates is always powerful. But at each of the transitional rites the "here" changes— *here* at the doors of the church (the threshold), *here* in the midst of the great assembly (the local church), *here* at the font of rebirth—and so does the "I." The catechumens are not being *introduced* to the bishop or to the assembly in any normal sense of that term. They are having their "I" spoken before God and in the midst of the great assembly through the mouth of the church. The testimony to God's grace— as that grace has been seen in the catechumens' lives and is now being confessed publicly by the godparents—makes this presentation what it is.

Enrollment of Names   The second main action of the rite is the enrollment of names. However the enrollment is carried out, it is undoubtedly the center of all the words and actions surrounding it. The bishop invites the elect to express their will in the matter, their assent, and then to "offer their names." After the enrollment, the act of election proclaims that the elect are now chosen. The instruction to the godparents gives them charge of the elect now that they have been enrolled. The gesture of laying a hand on the shoulder of one's candidate is a symbolic acceptance of this responsibility. The intercessions and a final prayer offered by the bishop with hands extended concludes the rite.

Even if the actual signing of the book of the elect is carried out at some other time, the enrollment stands as a   **21** gesture of crucial importance in this second part of the rite. A concession to the possible difficulties of inscribing all the names during the rite itself—the permission to write the names at some time prior to the rite of election—is no excuse for allowing the enrollment to appear vestigial or as an afterthought. Whenever the names are actually signed or written down, the *enrollment* of the catechumens takes place at the rite of election. If the way in which we celebrate election allows us to forget that, the basic shape of the rite is obscured. The weight of the enrollment in the tradition is comparable to that of the testimony, and the arrangement of the rite's structure reflects this.

Texts   The texts of the rite are quite restrained. There are no long orations; the dialogue with the godparents is brief and pithy. The presentation of the catechumens is quite dry, though there is freedom to adapt this introduction ("these or similar words"). The "admission" or "election" statement itself is admirably short and to the point. (The English of the 1988 version improves on the 1974 version, giving it the quality of a proclamation rather than that of a simple statement of fact, which could turn out to be rather limp in execution.) Unfortunately, the intercessions are couched in somewhat pedestrian language and include the prayer "that they may always remember this day of their election"—which, if the occasion is at all impressive, should take care of itself. Of course, intercessions are frequently adapted, but one would wish for more inspiring models all the same. Originally, the intercessions prayed for various graces for the elect,[2] but they were changed so that each petition would name one of the groups present at the rite (catechumens, godparents, catechists and so on).[3]

The closing prayer for the elect, offered by the bishop with hands outstretched, is undoubtedly the richest spoken text of the rite. It evokes the Old Testament background to election by its reference to "children of your promise." It evokes

St. Paul by its reference to adoption, and St. Augustine and the rest of the tradition of Western Christianity by its reference to being won not by nature but by grace.[4]

The weakness of the texts (in addition to what was already mentioned concerning the intercessions) is found in their tendency to overdo the explanatory material uttered by the bishop. Thus we have, for example, neither a ritual nor a rhetorical repetition but a redundancy when he addresses the catechumens after the testimony of godparents and then, later, in the act of election. The bishop says rather solemnly after this testimony that "the church in the name of Christ hereby calls you to the Easter sacraments." Then, after the enrollment, he expresses the same idea in the act of election. We also have a rubric for the celebrant to "explain briefly" the meaning of the rite of enrolling the names after it has taken place. As a preface to the examination of the candidates, the text the bishop speaks reviews what has transpired in the testimony of the godparents. The unfortunate effect is that the bishop appears to be making a running commentary on the ritual as it progresses.

Some of these occasions for the bishop to review what is going on are interpolations made at the suggestion of those who participated in the experimental stages of the development of the rites. The people who experimented with the rite in the field found that it was not well understood[5] and that "the true dimension of the intervention of the celebrant (eventually the bishop) is not apparent enough."[6] Among other things, it was proposed

> that the celebrant, by a concluding intervention [after the testimony of godparents], make the religious meaning of the church's decision appear. Through his judgment it is God himself who proclaims the catechumens worthy of approaching him, and consequently, of bringing him a new response.[7]

Does our present arrangement serve these noble purposes very well? It seems to me that the problems associated with "the intervention of the celebrant" have not yet been solved.

Of course, there is nothing wrong with having repetition in the rite. Liturgy relies on it, as does all great rhetoric. The great bishops of the patristic period could say a thing ten times without boring anybody, because they used metaphor—words that evoked pictures. But the unfortunate bishop of today is called on to deliver quite a few of these explanations without the help of robust imagery but rather in "churchy" language about sacraments, "favorable reports" and the like, thus earning Election's sorry reputation for "awards banquet" prose. The results are not memorable, though the moment seems to go on and on.

It is therefore a mercy that, on the whole, the catechumens can be expected to remember very little of what is said in a rite that concerns them. I, and many of my colleagues who have worked directly with catechumens, have learned this the hard way—by taking immense care in preparing texts and finding out later that the candidates barely heard a word. They do always, however, remember what *happened.* This does not mean that texts are unimportant; words we do not remember nonetheless have an impact on us. And words that are repeated from year to year have a cumulative effect on the faithful. But actions speak louder, at least initially, and are therefore of crucial concern to us.

Actions The actions described in the rite are few, however. The calling forward of the catechumens in their presentation is one action. The enrollment of names is another. The gesture made by the godparents toward the elect is the third. It is a challenge to planners to make the most of these actions while retaining their simplicity and to avoid the temptation of thinking that accretions will improve them. For the actions are definite, and each one speaks volumes, if done well. The art of celebration consists in knowing how to do them well and getting other things that might compete with them out of the way. The rite does not solve our logistical problems or teach us the art of celebration. But the structure it gives us has its own integrity.

Omissions There are a few things that the *editio typica* does not include that deserve mention. Although it allows that the baptized may take part in some of the rites of the catechumenate, as pastoral need suggests, it writes no versions of this rite for the baptized, nor does it provide a rite that would combine election with an analogous rite for the baptized. This is a case of the rite saying yes, a thing can be done, but not telling us how to do it.

The second lacuna is a bit different: The rites it offers for children of catechetical age do not include a Rite of Election. Here, the ritual structure envisioned for children is Rite of Acceptance, Scrutinies and initiation sacraments. This structure was immediately criticized in America for giving too much prominence to exorcism and thus to the phenomenon of sin. Since the 1988 American version added, with the approval of Rome, an optional Rite of Election for children, the objections to celebrating election with children could not have been strenuous. It is, however, a definite and obvious—and unexplained[8]—omission, which other studies may illuminate in ways that the present one cannot.

Last of all, though the *praenotanda* dutifully note that where the permanent diaconate exists, deacons have a role and a responsibility to assist with the catechumenate, the rubrics for the Rite of Election contain no role for deacons *per se.* Especially in election, because it is an episcopal rite, one would have expected the liturgy to include the normal role of the deacon. Nevertheless, the kinds of things that usually fall to the deacon—instructions, dismissals, intercessions, the reading of the gospel—never appear to be envisioned that way by the rubrics. Earlier drafts of the rites included the deacon explicitly, but the final version did not.

Adaptations and Developments in the United States

When the catechumenate first began to be implemented in this country following the release of the rite in English (1974), the celebration of all of the rites of initiation took place in the same setting: the parish. There was no diocesan Rite of Election for the simple reason that implementation did not begin first on the diocesan level. The direction that it was to be presided over "by the bishop or his delegate" was routinely ignored, usually for the best practical reason: If one waited for the bishop, one would wait a long time. And so, often without any formal delegation, the parish priest assumed the presider's role in this as in the other rites. The rite took place in the parish, within the Sunday assembly and within a more or less continuous stream of catechumenal rituals leading to the Easter Vigil. The features that distinguished it from the other initiation rites were its position in the church year at the head of Lent and the symbolic texts of the rite: the testimony of godparents, the book of the elect, the signing, the prayers. As more parishes began to use the adult initiation rites, however, it became feasible for the bishop himself to preside at the Rite of Election, and diocesan personnel worked toward this end.

From Parochial to Diocesan Celebration　The mid-1980s saw the widespread development across the country of diocesan celebrations of the Rite of Election. With this concrete shift in polity several things happened. First of all, the diocesan bishop (and later, auxiliary bishops, in those dioceses that have them) was brought into more direct contact with the catechumenate than he had hitherto enjoyed. This contact was still quite attenuated, and in some cases entirely limited to this annual liturgical event; but it was an improvement over no contact at all or impressions formed by hearsay. In fact, it is probably this contact more than any other that served to move the episcopate in this country from a position of relative indifference to the catechumenate to one of support and even enthusiasm for it. It called the bishops' attention to the fledgling catechumenate and presented it in a positive light. In the near-complete absence of routine pastoral visits by bishops to catechumenate groups in parishes, not to mention the rarity of parish catechumenate group visits to the cathedral of the diocese, the diocesan Rite of Election in most places also assumed the distinction of being the catechumens' and candidates' first face-to-face encounter with their bishop, as well as the first time they set foot in the cathedral.

Meanwhile, responsibility for the planning of this liturgical event shifted from parish to diocesan personnel. Even in places where diocesan personnel relied on volunteers from parishes to assist in the preparations for this rite, a set of supraparochial concerns that diocesan personnel represent necessarily came into prominence when the bishop presided at a diocesan liturgy. Diocesan personnel therefore normally took the ultimate responsibility for planning and evaluating this liturgy.

As the rite migrated from the parish church to the cathedral, or to some other diocesan site chosen for the occasion, the assembly also changed. No longer was the assembly primarily a gathering of the faithful from the parish, of those who had taken part in the earlier stages of these particular catechumens' ritual initiation and who shared a set of concrete particulars with them in their regular parish liturgy (such as language, locale, musical repertoire, "style" and so on). Rather, it became an assembly of groups, in some cases quite heterogeneous groups at that. Each group consisted of those most directly involved in the work of the catechumenate in each parish: sponsors, godparents, catechists, family members, friends, clergy and so on, known to one another but unknown to those in the other groups.

Development of Rites of Sending   In answer to the loss felt in the parish when the celebration of election moved to a diocesan setting, a parish ritual anticipating (and in certain respects duplicating) the Rite of Election was devised by Americans and accepted by Rome as an official adaptation for the United States—the Rite of Sending Catechumens to Election.[9] The *editio typica* makes it clear that if the Rite of Election for any reason does not include the calling out of individual names, such an action must take place in another setting. While this directive provides a warrant for having such a preliminary rite, the Rite of Sending is rarely (if ever) viewed as an occasion for the calling of names. Its purpose is to allow the parish community to express its "approval" and "care and support" (RCIA, #107) of the catechumens.

The Rite of Sending Catechumens to Election and Candidates to the Call to Continuing Conversion was devised as the parish companion liturgy to the combined Rite of Election and Call to Continuing Conversion that is celebrated on a diocesan level. The Rite of Sending to the Call to Continuing Conversion was coined for the case of candidates only. In both of these rites of sending, the candidates receive only the briefest affirmation by the sponsors and assembly, presumably to underscore the difference between their status and that of the catechumens, who are ordinarily the subject of a more extensive testimony by their godparents. (Why the candidates are permitted to have an even longer testimony than the catechumens do at election itself but *not* in the Rite of Sending is a mystery, especially because the very content of the testimony presumably distinguishes the two groups; but this is how the American adaptation is written.)

Although these rites are different from one another in certain respects, it makes sense for our purposes to refer to them all collectively as one adaptation: the Rite of Sending. Sending has been widely used since the publication of the 1988 version of the RCIA. Some would even argue that election itself is incomplete without a parish Rite of Sending.

Separation from the First Sunday of Lent   The Rite of Election has also migrated out of its original context in the eucharist of the First Sunday of Lent. Nowhere to my knowledge is a diocesan Rite of Election held in the context of Mass at all, which is its principal setting according to the rite itself. To do so in a diocesan liturgy would raise difficult practical questions, such as how to dismiss multitudes of catechumens, whether or not the candidates should go with them, and to what extent all this would duplicate the parish liturgy of the First Sunday of Lent or compete with it.

The practical accommodation offered in the rite, and generally followed, is to hold the Rite of Election as a part of a liturgy of the word. As dioceses are faced with the swelling numbers that require the scheduling of multiple celebrations of the rite, there also has been an increasing movement away from celebrating the Rite of Election uniquely on the First Sunday of Lent. Having several celebrations usually means that one is held on the First Sunday of Lent and others are held on weekdays close to that time. To make this scenario complete, once these other changes have taken place, other readings are frequently substituted for those of the First Sunday of Lent. Thus the break from the Mass of the First Sunday of Lent is often fairly complete.

This break, when accompanied by a change in the readings, signifies more than a mere change of schedule. The readings of the First Sunday of Lent provide a rich context of interpretation for understanding the meaning of the Rite of Election. Cut adrift from its moorings in these readings, the rite can float in any number of directions. The meaning of the rite is reshaped by the selection of different readings. Often enough, planners are not even aware that the readings assigned for the First Sunday of Lent have anything to do with election, and so will easily give them up. I hope to show that this move is ill-advised and that the readings are in fact speaking directly out of a theological perspective on election.

Other Developments   While these changes of an external and practical nature have been taking place, other important developments have occurred in our pastoral practice and thinking about the rite as well. One of these was occasioned by the unofficial introduction into the rite (in some dioceses, not all) of an entirely new ritual element, known neither to the tradition nor to the present text: having the bishop shake each catechumen's or candidate's hand, either at the presentation of the candidates or after the enrollment of names. This individual, personal contact by the bishop has been clearly and unambiguously intended to convey hospitality. It is not associated with the examination of the catechumens or the testimony of the godparents, as was the presentation of catechumens to the bishop one by one in Egeria's account of such a liturgy in Jerusalem. It is not a blessing or a dismissal. It is informally described as "meeting the bishop" and, alternatively, as "being welcomed by the bishop."

While not universally adopted, this new element has enjoyed some popularity and is even considered by some to be the centerpiece of their experience of the rite. One cannot ask strongly enough what the proper role of the bishop is in this rite. We will look at this question with some care. For most catechumens (and candidates) the Rite of Election (and Call to Continuing Conversion) is the only ritual of their catechumenate over which the bishop presides. One also might well inquire to what extent the rite is about the bishop. To what extent do our concerns about the bishop get in the way of the rite being about anything else?

We have also witnessed the development of a rationale for the diocesan rite that makes explicit use of the supra-parochial setting as a catechetical tool, which is to say that people have begun to look at election as a lesson in belonging to the universal church, an introduction into a diocesan community, or a welcome into a church larger than the parish. This lesson uses a concrete, shared experience that often spontaneously generates a powerful impression upon the individual. It is also a selling point for overcoming a more or less natural parochialism that keeps people at home in their parishes and leads them to resist the invitation to a diocesan gathering. It is not unusual to find reflections on the meaning of the diocesan Rite of Election dominated by awe at the numbers of initiates, wonder at the beauty of the cathedral church, and surprise at the scope of the diocese. Does all this have anything to do with election?

Another development has been the virtual extinction of debate concerning the baptized candidates' proper place at this juncture in the process, with the possible exception of the question of whether it is appropriate for them to sign the Book of the Elect. The practice of having godparents sign the book along with the elect has disappeared pretty much without a trace since the new text emerged in 1988 (although it is allowed by the 1988 text); but the question of whether the baptized candidates should sign remains a disputed issue, in spite of clear and unambiguous directions by the national statutes that they should not. Yet even this question appears to be fading. In the spring 1992 Forum *Newsletter,* North American Forum president Jim Dunning mounted a defense of the thesis that candidates should be treated like catechumens in this rite and in the Scrutinies. His challenge to "take me on," generated only eight letters, **31** and he reported in the Winter 1993 issue that all of the letters were sympathetic to his position. Those opposed were apparently not inclined to fight, because their position is defended by the National Statutes. But because the ground of the fight is presumably the importance of maintaining certain symbolic connections between baptism itself and the rites of the catechumenate, one wonders a bit at the silence.

All of the possible venues given by the rite for the signing of the book of the elect have been tried, with no resulting consensus but with very little bloodshed either. Local custom is being formed diocese by diocese and parish by parish. In some places the signing takes place at the cathedral. In others, it takes place at the parish during the Rite of Sending. In some cases the book is signed at the altar; in others, on a book stand. After the rite, the book may be enshrined in a special place in the church or cathedral, or not, as the case may be. Rhetoric about the Book of the Elect that has picked up and used biblical references to "the book of life" (references that have a long history in the tradition concerning election) has tended to color the discussion about who signs the book.

Some dioceses, perhaps feeling that the absence of any signing in the cathedral rite is a bad thing or that something more on the part of the bishop is required than just receiving the names of the elect, have invented the practice of having the bishop sign his own name in the Book of the Elect. This is a complete novelty, unknown to the rite itself and unknown to any tradition pertaining to this juncture in Christian initiation. Some have speculated that the practice arose from publishers having put a line for the bishop at the bottom of each page of the book. While this seems rather scant warrant for inventing a new liturgical practice, it is not impossible that it developed in this way. A serious meaning has been attached to this gesture, however: It is sometimes described as having the bishop "ratify" what takes place in the election.

The people who participate in the Rite of Election usually comprise many different categories according to their catechetical preparation, age, cultural background and so on. This variety adds richness and also some complexities to the celebration of the rite.

The range of catechetical background that the catechumens and candidates bring to this event is generally quite wide. At the top of the scale, one sees representatives from catechumenates who have labored long and hard at the question of discernment. The degree to which a parish has grappled seriously with discernment of readiness is probably the surest sign of how deeply the work of the catechumenate has been grasped. Serious discernment usually only appears in conjunction with a year-round catechumenate accompanied by well-developed ministries and stable leadership. As a result, the catechumens and candidates coming with such groups are typically mature in their intention, and they know what is going on.

One also sees represented those catechumenates that are operating on a school-year model, all of whose catechumens and candidates "graduate" without question once Lent comes around. Not necessarily any less enthusiastic or earnest than the first group, such catechumens and candidates are nonetheless typically at a disadvantage because of having had only a few months of catechesis. The question of "what is a bishop?" might be more pressing to them than "what is election?"

And one sees the groups that are scraped up at the last minute by pastors who have neglected to do anything by way of a catechumenate prior to the announcement of this rite, with its threatening overtones of episcopal authority. (The scraped-up catechumenate group, though hardly ideal, is not without historical precedent. Michel Dujarier claims that the building up of catechumenal use of the lenten period, which election inaugurates, was actually a last-ditch attempt by fifth-century bishops to salvage catechumenal formation that had fallen on hard times after 313.)[10]   **33**

Catechumens and candidates of the last category typically do not even know that they are catechumens and candidates, let alone what election means.

Due to the American view that the Rite of Election is also suitable for children of catechetical age, it is more and more common to see children at this rite. As we have already seen, the *editio typica,* appropriately or not, has no celebration of election for children. The adaptations for the United States include a Rite of Election for children, which is to be superseded by the adult rite in the case of mixed groups. In practice thus far, this has meant that, in most cases, the cathedral celebrations have followed the adult rite. But in any event, more children are now participating in the rite with the adults.

Normally the full cultural and economic diversity of the local church will be in evidence at the Rite of Election. And participation will mean different things to different people. The diverse cultures, classes and races of people expected in a diocesan gathering in any but the most homogeneous of regions inevitably bring along with them, implicitly, a whole array of pressing social questions. By this I mean questions of identity, status and integration within the community of the church—questions that gather considerable force from whatever the prevailing winds are outside the church. Such questions rightfully concern the whole body of the church and are present even if they are not explicitly acknowledged. Especially in urban dioceses, but also in any diocese that is ethnically and racially heterogeneous, one comes face-to-face with the fact that our church is made up not only of individuals but of peoples. The people of God are indeed irreducibly "elect of every nation."

Summary A situation of immense complexity confronts us when we approach the Rite of Election today. What started out as a rite for adult catechumens, presided over by the bishop at the Mass of the First Sunday of Lent, has mushroomed into a complicated constellation of events embracing myriad categories of persons and places, and generating multiple meanings along the way. Some of these developments must be affirmed. Others deserve to be questioned.

The one development that has not been seen at all is a more careful pastoral and theological reflection on the meaning of divine election, both broadly for the church and more narrowly for the catechumenate. This development might have come about in increased attention to what the scriptures, both those assigned for the Mass of the day and generally, have to say about God's election. It might have emerged in the guise of more reflection on just what the texts and symbols of the rite itself have to do with election. It might have taken the form of more catechists delving into the questions and conflicts that gave the Catholic doctrine of election its characteristic shape and then asking what insights this brings into what it means to be a Catholic Christian today.

But none of this delving, questioning or sifting has happened. My impression is that our pastoral practice has distracted us from asking these kinds of questions and that bishops, having one shot at preaching to this population, are speaking about initiation in much more general terms. And the rite as we have developed, adapted and changed it is increasingly unlikely to suggest to us that we should do otherwise.

We have taken the "election" aspect of the Rite of Election lightly, almost as if it is an accident that the ritual bears that name. Rather than wrestle with the more difficult aspects of a doctrine that frankly challenges both our implicit religious pluralism and triumphalism, we have settled for a vague notion that election is a kind of ecclesial version of personal affirmation: "I am special." Then, when we arrive at a rite in which the main ritual action is a handshake with the bishop, and everyone is taking it for granted that the purpose of our gathering is to offer a "welcome to the larger church," we do not really notice that something is missing. The circle of affirmation is complete. Everyone loved being made to feel welcome at this great, big, wonderful liturgy. They went home thrilled. Who would want to think about the theological implications of election in the face of such a good experience? The fact that the readings of the First Sunday of Lent, with their tales of primordial disaster, costly redemption from sin, and satanic temptations in a desert appear as strangers in the midst of all this wonder of hospitality and personal affirmation does not detain us long. We simply change the readings.

Chapter 3

The Theology of Election

■

Election is surely one of the weightiest concepts in scripture and in subsequent Christian theology. Jacques Guillet writes that "Without election it is impossible to understand anything about God's plan and will. . . . It is the entirety of redemption; it is the fullness of scripture."[1] Next to covenant, and intimately related to it, the concept of election is perhaps the most decisive one for the religion of Israel.[2] And for the Christian, the idea that Jesus is the elect of God and the idea that the church is elect in Christ are fundamental.[3] Election has been called "the heart of the church."[4]

The specifically Christian tradition surrounding election is formidable. St. Paul's wrestling with the question of the election of the Gentiles has had important consequences for Christian theology and for our self-definition in relation to the Jewish people. St. Augustine's writings on election, specifically against the Pelagian and Semi-Pelagian heresies,[5] have played an important role in the development of the doctrine of grace in the Western church. Debates about election, which began around the time of the Reformation and continued through the early eighteenth century—not only those of the Catholics against the Lutherans, the Calvinists and the Jansenists, but also between the Molinists and the Thomists, between the Lutherans and the theologians of the Reformed Churches, and between the Reformed and the Remonstrants and Arminians—hammered out refinements and variations of positions that served as key issues of contention between churches and between schools of thought within churches for centuries.

The doctrine of election is still extraordinarily productive in Reformed theology,[6] and though the concept of election is not a favorite subject of contemporary Roman Catholic systematic theologians,[7] it claims considerable attention in the field of biblical theology across confessional lines. Although certainly not all of the arguments and distinctions raised in these many discussions will be relevant to our purposes here, they do show that what one believes about election has long been taken seriously by Western Christians.

Given all of this, it is disappointing that at least one contemporary writer on the catechumenate should find it necessary in commenting on the Rite of Election to clarify that "election" in this case is not an affair of the ballot box.[8] Yet it is no doubt necessary in our secular age to remind people that election can mean something other than the vote. Unfortunately, for many Catholics today the term *election* does not call up the many scriptural and theological associations that it once did. Many Catholics do not even know that there is a Catholic doctrine of election. They associate the theological concept of election exclusively with Calvinism—and various debased forms of Calvinism, at that—and have a very unfavorable impression of it indeed. Yet if election is as important as I wish to argue that it is, we do well to leave aside our preconceptions and take a fresh look at it, especially as it appears in scripture.

By attending to the election of Israel, the election of Jesus and the election of the church, as they emerge from the witness of scripture, we will be in a better position to discover what election has to do with Christian initiation.

Israel's Election

Israel's consciousness of being elect, the chosen people[9] of YHWH, permeates the entire Old Testament. One can discern the influence of this belief in every epoch of Israel's history. "Though given its clearest expression and characteristic vocabulary in literature of the seventh and sixth centuries [BC]," writes John Bright, "the notion of election was dominant in Israel's faith from the beginning."[10] The life of the chosen people began with the election of the patriarch Abraham, which is recounted in the book of Genesis. The life of this people in relation to God, through all the epochs of its history, is the focus of most of the Old Testament.

There is no question that the making of the Mosaic covenant and the events surrounding it are central to the understanding of Israel's election. Though the scriptures viewed the early history of the people in light of its election, the events par excellence that constituted Israel as the chosen people are described in the Old Testament accounts of the Exodus and the wandering in the wilderness. Throughout the Old Testament these events are recalled and celebrated because they forged the identity of the chosen people. Yet it would be a mistake to think that the meaning of election is exhaustively presented in the texts relating to the exodus and the wandering in the desert, and that other texts merely repeat the formulas of the book of Deuteronomy. On the contrary, while key themes are revisited, important insights that are somewhat indistinct in Deuteronomy are brought into focus by the treatment given election in other quarters—the accounts of the primeval and early history in Genesis, the history of the monarchy in the books of Samuel and Kings, the prophetic literature and the psalms, to name a few. It is desirable to **39** seek a sense of the whole as much as possible for the balance and overall integrity that the full witness provides.

For example, it is the primeval and early history that places election in the framework of a universal context. In the history of Israel's monarchy, God's election of individuals comes to light in particular ways, especially in the election of David and the special relationship that God has to the Davidic monarchy. The chilling reality of election as the basis for divine judgment against Israel, and the freedom of God to withdraw this election, can be seen in the prophetic writings. The eschatological meaning of Israel's election emerges in the prophetic writings as well. Elect individuals who appear in the prophetic literature, such as the prophets and the "suffering servant," enhance our understanding of election. Last of all, the doxological dimensions of election are only fully appreciated by having recourse to the psalms. The fact that Israel relates to "the electing God" in prayer and praise, in thanksgiving and petition, tells us something important about election without which our understanding would be incomplete.

Of course nothing like the whole can be described, much less detailed, in a short treatment such as this. I have chosen therefore to examine only two areas of the Old Testament witness concerning election, as a way to limit the discussion to points that will be most useful for considering the strands of the biblical doctrine of election that appear in the lectionary readings for the First Sunday of Lent. Though I will at times make references to other points as well, these two areas will make up the greater part of our considerations. These areas are those surrounding the call of Abraham and the Exodus, both of which are important to the other stages of the catechumenate journey as well.[11]

The Relationship of Israel to the Nations The individual stories contained in the book of Genesis are familiar enough when taken in isolation from one another, but when seen together, they form a larger pattern that makes a major point concerning God's relationship to the human race.[12] By taking the early chapters of Genesis in broad outline, we see that they unfold a story of sin and grace that leads up to the election of the chosen people.

In creation, God's word brings forth out of chaos and the abyss the world and all its living creatures in their tremendous beauty, order and goodness. The creation is crowned by human beings, whom God fashions out of the clay of the ground and into whom he breathes his spirit. But Adam and Eve turn away from this beneficent God. Their sin results in judgment; they are expelled from the garden. Thereafter, disorder and strife mark relations between the sexes, the earth will not yield its fruit except to painful toil, suffering and death become inevitable, and intimacy with God is lost. But God has mercy on them, even in this judgment. God clothes Adam and Eve when they leave the garden—a protective gesture. The story is one of catastrophe, but the last word is God's grace.

When Cain kills his brother Abel, God's wrath is justly roused again. "Your brother's blood cries out to me from the soil!" the Lord says (Genesis 4:10). Violence and bloodshed provoke God's anger and judgment. The punishment of a new exile—recalling the expulsion from the garden of Eden—falls upon Cain, and he is sent to wander all his days. But God does not abandon Cain. God sets a mark upon Cain so that he will not be killed. God's mercy gives Cain protection beyond what he deserves, and the story ends this way—not in judgment, but in mercy.

Evil continues to appear anew, however, in the brutality of Lamech, in the marriage of women with angels (which signals a kind of illegitimate disintegration of the boundaries between heaven and earth),[13] and finally in the conditions that lead God to destroy the earth by means of the great flood.

The story of Noah begins with an account of how the sinfulness of the people of the earth has not abated but only multiplied and grown. What God sees when he looks upon the world he so lovingly created is such evil and wickedness that "the Lord was sorry that he had made [humanity] on the earth, and it grieved him to his heart" (Genesis 6:6). Destruction comes over the earth by means of the flood, as God's judgment falls again. The story of the flood is told both as a terrible downpour of forty days' duration, and—much more frighteningly—as the rolling back of the restraints that God had placed on the waters in creation: "All the fountains of the great abyss burst forth, and the floodgates of the sky were opened" (Genesis 7:11).[14] The flood is a terrifying, cataclysmic disaster. Yet it is not the flood but the rainbow and the covenant that end the story. God's promise never again to destroy the earth concludes this tale of disaster with the promise of hope.

What follows next is an impressive listing of all the peoples of the earth that descended from the family of Noah. This passage—sometimes called the "table of the nations"—gives a panoramic view of all the peoples of the world raised up in this new beginning by God's mercy. What is perhaps most striking about this table of the nations, however, is that one looks in vain for Israel among the peoples listed there. In a certain sense Israel is present in the form of a people that was ancestral to Israel, but no attention is paid to this whatsoever. It would have been so easy for Israel to write in a prominent role for itself at this point in the narrative. The glorious display of the fruitfulness of the human race after the flood could have been the occasion for Israel to emerge as the star of the new creation: special to God from the beginning, in the midst of all the nations, the way it was meant to be. But Israel is nowhere to be found.

The last episode of the primal history, following this table of the nations, is the story of the Tower of Babel. What began as evidence of the greatness of God—the people themselves, splendid in their diversity and united by a single language—is turned toward works of presumption, arrogance and vain ambition. The citizens of Babel build a tower, "to make a name for ourselves" (Genesis 11:4), and in an act of judgment God shatters their language so that they no longer can understand one another. There the story ends. And so we are left at last with an unrelieved disaster: The great riches of God's creation, represented by all the nations, now "bear the deep scars of God's judging intervention."[15] There is no mitigation.

The Tower of Babel therefore raises the question: Is God's mercy finally exhausted? Babel sets up and draws the whole of the primal history into focus in what may be called the problem of the nations. Then, having set up this wrenching problem—this bankruptcy of the human race, this specter of multiplicity and power turned to chaos and isolation rather than solidarity and peace—the scriptures suddenly shift from universal concerns of creation, sin, the sexes, language and so on, to one man, one family and one nation through whom "all the communities of the earth shall find blessing" (Genesis 12:3).

The word that God speaks against the background of Babel, and indeed against the background of the whole recurring pattern of sin and judgment in the primal history, is the call of Abraham. The election of Israel must be seen therefore as God's unwillingness to give up on the world, God's refusal to accept the "no" that the human race has been offering since the beginning of time. The promises made to Abraham and the love that God lavishes on Israel are to become the means by which God's goodness may be shown to the world that has rejected him. The election of Israel does not represent the scaling down of divine expectations—although we cannot save everyone, let us at least save a few—but rather a new and bold initiative on God's part for those who have eyes to see it.

The Chosen People   If the early chapters of Genesis give us a vision of the broad context of God's election of   **43**

Israel, the scriptures dealing with the Exodus give us the "inside" of that corporate experience of being chosen. The people of Israel spoke about what it meant to be God's elect most eloquently in the language of the book of Deuteronomy. It was to be delivered from slavery in Egypt with great "signs and wonders" (Deuteronomy 4:34), to be saved by God's "mighty hand" and "outstretched arm" (Deuteronomy 5:15). It was to stand at the foot of the smoking mountain and receive God's holy law (Deuteronomy 4:11–14), to hear the words of the greatest of all prophets, to know God's name. It was to choose between life and death, for themselves and for their children (Deuteronomy 30:19), to bind themselves in covenant with the One who had chosen them. It was to undertake an arduous journey through a wilderness in hopes of reaching a promised land. It was to know God as the One who acts—not according to the rhythms of the circling seasons, nor in answer to his own needs, nor yet as agent of human wants or designs—but in freedom and out of love. They rejoiced in their election as an unmerited gift of God.

For while the people of Israel confessed the greatness of God and his power over all the created world, they just as readily confessed to their own weakness and smallness among all the nations of the world. Indeed, they emphasized it. Their election was not to be confused with nationalism or ethnic pride, but was favor bestowed on them for God's purposes and to God's glory. In the words of Yehezkel Kaufmann:

> Israel's national prowess was not sacred or divine; divine was the favor, YHWH's presence, the election to be a vehicle of YHWH's manifestation. . . . Small, weak and powerless in itself, Israel's success attests the power of YHWH; its history is thus a wonder and a sign, the actualization of God's word and will. This alone was the purpose of its election.[16]

Israel's election called the people to the privileges and responsibilities of living the covenant life and therefore called them to the service of God,[17] borne out in concrete circumstances. A free response was called for. When the covenant was set before them, the people were asked to choose. Then through this covenant, God exercised a claim on the elect that influenced their lives through the many forms that the covenant took: the ordering of personal conduct, family life, prayer, community life, and the cult of their worship. What Karl Barth says of election generally is abundantly borne out by Israel's election: "Our return to obedience is indeed the aim of free grace. It is for this that it makes us free. . . . The mystery of the election of God is the summons to obedience."[18] The claim of election, realized in the covenant, calls the chosen people to praise and serve God: not only to be God's own, but also to act rightly before him.

God's election is astonishing, according to the biblical witness, because he bestows it on the weakest and smallest of peoples. Its "natural condition" makes Israel the least likely people to become the bearer of the revelation of the Most High God. Yet Israel is chosen.

The proper response of the people (which does not always follow in fact, but is always held forth as normative) is humility and joy—a sense of privilege that leads not to self-aggrandizement but to praise of the One who gives the privilege. Pride is incompatible with a proper grasp of the meaning of election; so is any shadow of the notion that Israel enjoys special claims upon God because of its election.

The status that the people are given and the benefits that they receive from the covenant are entirely in the hands of God, who can take them back and who is not bound to them as if by a higher law or some sense of their inherent fitness. God's faithfulness to the covenant thus is also seen as a gracious act, commensurate with the greatness of his act of election, which is, above all, an act of self-giving love.

It is important to emphasize that election cannot be understood as a species of what modern psychology would call "affirmation." It is not based on any intrinsic merits of the one elected. As we have already seen, the goal of election is not the realization of the identity of the group but the achievement of God's will for the world. It does not inevitably lead to the building up of confidence in one's self; rather, it leads to the building up of confidence in God. It is an entirely theocentric concept.

The experience of election for the people of Israel consisted as much of challenge, moral struggle and judgment as it did of the grateful reception of an embracing and nurturing love. For all these reasons, it would be a serious reduction of the theological concept of election to attempt to assimilate it into the psychological concept of affirmation.[19] Election contains within itself some kinds of affirmation, but election remains the much wider and richer concept.

Election in the New Testament

The New Testament supports the notion that the followers of Christ are the heirs to the election of Israel, much in the manner of a "faithful remnant" (Romans 11:5).[20] But what they inherit is not a simple continuity with the historical people of Israel. Rather, they inherit the reign of God, the life of the Age to Come[21] — an eschatological inheritance. This inheritance is realized not only at the final judgment, but in the present time, as the gospel is preached to the whole world.

The Reign of God Is at Hand The first Christians regarded the coming of Christ as a crisis, a turning point in history as well as a turning point for the individual. With the coming of Christ, the reign of God is truly at hand; the Age to Come has arrived. Although a final judgment will also come, the last days are already here. Application of the word *election* to the church in the New Testament is both informed by the contours of the Old Testament concept of election and invariably stamped by these eschatological convictions.

Thus, Jesus chooses the twelve (Luke 6:13)—clearly the election of Israel is recalled here—but he sends them out to exorcise, heal and proclaim the reign of God (Luke 9:1, 2). It is an eschatological mission, continued in the Acts of the Apostles. In the spirit of this preaching mission, Paul is chosen (Acts 9:15), Matthias is chosen to replace Judas (Acts 1:24), and Stephen and six others are chosen for service (Acts 6:5). In the latter cases, when the apostles choose, they do so under the guidance of the Holy Spirit, the outpouring of which is a hallmark of the messianic era.[22] In John's gospel, Jesus says to his disciples, "It was not you who chose me; it was I who chose you to go forth and bear fruit" (John 15:16). Here, as in the Old Testament, the initiative of election is all on one side. But the divine initiative here belongs to Jesus himself, and its result is that those who are chosen experience a definitive break from the world (John 15:19) even as they go about their mission in the world.

Election involves God's protection of the elect through every circumstance of trial. At the final consummation, God will gather the elect from the four winds (Matthew 24:31, Mark 13:27); he will shorten the final days for them so that they will not be destroyed (Matthew 24:22, Mark 13:20). They will be endangered by false messiahs and false prophets before the end comes, but will persevere (Matthew 24:24, Mark 13:22). God will vindicate them with his just judgments (Luke 18:7, Romans 8:33) and will bring them into glory (Revelation 17:14); the chosen are those who come to the Messianic banquet (Matthew 22:14). The expression "chosen in Christ" (Ephesians 1:4) is reminiscent of Jewish apocalyptic literature, which speaks of a messianic deliverer, called "the Elect," who is king of the whole company of heaven and in whom all are gathered up.[23] And indeed, that these are chosen before the world began establishes them in a destiny that is eternal.

The Church Is the Elect of God   The church is referred to as the elect in various ways that call to mind both the Old Testament background of election and New Testament eschatology. God's election not only is bestowed freely on unworthy people, it effects the reversals characteristic of the gospel of the reign of God: The weak and foolish of the world are chosen to shame the strong and wise (1 Corinthians 1:27–28), and God chooses the poor (James 2:5). The people of the church addressed in 1 Peter "in these last days" are called "the elect" (1 Peter 1:2; 2:9) and also "the people of God," which is a standard Old Testament usage for the chosen people.

"The elect," simply as a designation for the baptized, also carries an eschatological tone. The Apostle bears with suffering in order that "the elect" may obtain *eternal* glory (2 Timothy 2:10) and promotes their knowledge of the truth in hopes of their attaining *everlasting* life (Titus 1:1–2). The whole local church community is personified as "the elect lady" who brings forth children as the fruit of faithfulness to the gospel (2 John 1, 13).[24] God's chosen are "holy and beloved" (Colossians 3:12) and so must conduct themselves according to virtues that closely resemble the gifts of the Spirit. They are urged to be zealous about making their call and election secure (2 Peter 1:10).

Jesus Is the Elect of God   Jesus himself is designated as the elect of God in several key places in the New Testament. John the baptist identifies Jesus as the elect of God at his baptism (John 1:31),[25] and within the Johannine presentation of Jesus' work as a kind of "courtroom drama"[26] in which the world is brought to judgment, the appearance of Jesus as the elect of God in John the Baptist's opening deposition is particularly powerful.

In Luke's gospel, Jesus is identified as the elect of God at his transfiguration (Luke 9:35) and on the cross (23:35). In the first instance, the glory and impending suffering of

Christ are joined together.[27] The passage shows that the elect of God is this man Jesus, who is to suffer and be glorified. Taken in connection with it, the passage at the very event of his crucifixion—which bystanders mock as a demonstration of God's rejection—is especially striking.[28] The two passages together, by pointing out that God's elect (Christ crucified) is rejected by the leaders of the Jewish people, opens the way for the church to be identified as the faithful remnant of Israel.[29]

Other direct references to the election of Jesus are found in the first letter of Peter (1 Peter 2:4, 6). Here, the author contrasts the worthiness of God's elect, Jesus, with the folly of those who reject this chosen one of God. Jesus is "a living stone, rejected by men but approved *(eklektos),* nonetheless, and precious in God's eyes" (1 Peter 2:4). The author goes on to quote from the prophet Isaiah (28:16):[30] "See, I am laying a cornerstone in Zion, an approved *(eklektos)* stone, and precious. He who puts his faith in it shall not be shaken" (1 Peter 2:6). He asserts that this is a stone "which the builders rejected that became a cornerstone" (Psalm 118:22; see also Matthew 21:42, Acts 4:11) and that it is a stumbling block to those who do not believe in God's word.[31] What God has done in his chosen one, Jesus, has decisive significance. It is the occasion either for the founding of steadfast faith in those who believe or for the downfall of those who refuse to believe. The passage is hortatory; it urges its readers to found their faith upon Christ.

It is particularly interesting for our purposes to note that 1 Peter is full of allusions to Christian baptism and that large parts of the letter are even considered by some scholars to have been taken substantially from an early Christian baptismal liturgy.[32] The church accords special honor to the First Letter of Peter by having portions of it read every Sunday of the Easter season during Year A of the lectionary. Paragraph 247 of the *Rite of Christian Initiation of Adults* in turn calls attention to the benefits of this set of Easter season readings for the neophytes' Masses and mystagogy.

A reading from 1 Peter also appears in the lectionary for Year B on the First Sunday of Lent. In short, 1 Peter contains some very important texts for Christian initiation. It is appropriate, therefore, that we find in it several references to election, both of Christ and of the church.

Beyond these instances where the actual word *election* is used in the New Testament, there is abundant material to suggest ways in which Jesus stands in the tradition of election described in the Old Testament. The material for reflection here is so copious that we cannot consider it all in detail. Therefore we will unfold the content of only one example that is particularly relevant to the lectionary for the First Sunday of Lent and will otherwise simply mention the categories into which the material falls.

The New Testament presents Jesus as both inheriting and epitomizing the election of the chosen people. A particularly good example of this can be found in the gospel readings of the First Sunday of Lent. The sojourn of Jesus for forty days in the wilderness recalls the forty years that the chosen people spent in the desert—a time of testing, in which their identity was formed. The temptations of Jesus recall the tests to which the chosen people were subjected: their physical hunger for bread, the temptation to test God and the lure of idolatry. The synoptic accounts of Jesus' temptations in the desert tell the story of Jesus' own life-determining choices: to embrace God's word, to trust God humbly and to worship God alone. Given the Old Testament background, these decisions in the face of Satan's temptations stand out as Jesus' "yes" to his election. The character of his whole public ministry in some sense flows from these fundamental decisions. They show that he is the one in whom the grace of election will be realized to perfection. Thus, in narrative form, the story of Jesus' temptations in the desert presents us with crucial insights into his election and our own.

In addition to epitomizing the election of the whole people of Israel, Jesus stands in other important Old

Testament traditions concerning election as well. The New Testament identifies Jesus with the line of David and the Davidic kingship. Jesus the Son of King David is Jesus the elect king, who reigns by God's choice. The New Testament also identifies Jesus with the suffering servant of Deutero-Isaiah, another chosen individual of the Old Testament whose particular obedience to God produces salvific consequences that are universal in their scope.

Election involves the scandal of particularity. We see that this is true of Jesus in great measure. God has a unique relationship with Jesus; it is through this one particular person that humanity and creation receive God's self-communication. At his baptism, at his transfiguration and on the cross, Jesus is singled out as the object of divine favor. The connection of election with these gestures of divine approbation is unmistakable.

Divine election confounds human pride. The lowliness of Jesus in worldly terms—his humility, his poverty—conform to this profile exactly. The servanthood of Jesus, his obedience even unto death, his prayer and his attitude toward God make him the exemplar of the right response to the electing God.

Election and the Catechumenate

One of the problems of the church in our time is that the church is so often turned in on itself. The work of maintaining our identity and institutions, effecting internal renewal and wrestling with intramural problems can be very absorbing. Consequently, initiation into the community of faith often—too often—means initiation into a community turned inward, initiation into a church that is not in any significant sense a church of mission. If this is the mindset that is brought to Christian initiation, the inevitable corollary is that to be God's chosen is to climb into the cocoon of church community, to get on the glory train before it leaves the station, to "find myself" in the Catholic church. These are human projects, and they are absorbing ones. They arise from pressing needs for protection, affirmation, honor and self-esteem—none of which are bad things. But they are not the end for which the people of God is elected.

Only a church turned outward in mission can initiate new members into such an outward-directed vision as the one we see in the gospels. While the universal significance of God's action in electing the chosen people is implicit in the Old Testament texts concerning election, it must be admitted that Judaism rarely gave evidence of such a missionary emphasis. It was Christianity that picked up and brought forward the connection between election and mission in its passion to preach the gospel to all nations. In the language of the New Testament, the followers of Jesus are called to be light and salt for the world. Such a vision is presumed by the documents of the catechumenate.

We have already seen how closely the language of election in the New Testament is connected with eschatology. The first Christians were convinced that the coming of Christ was a crisis, a definitive turning point in history, the continuing reality of which is mediated by the Holy Spirit. That this conviction exercised a profound effect on Christian baptism is beyond question.[33] That the Rite of Election, within the broad sweep of the order of Christian initiation of adults, should in various ways call to mind the reign of God, the end times and eternal stakes, is therefore altogether fitting. The "book of life" metaphor for the Book of the Elect is appropriate. And a consciousness of Spirit-filled mission rightly informs both the vision of the church and the goals of the catechumenate.

The obedience to which the elect are called, the "covenant life" (if we may so designate our communal existence in the church under the Spirit) to which the elect are called, is both for their own salvation and for the mission of the church. The two are inextricably united. So, of course, moral conversion is essential to the catechumenate; and, of course, apostolic works are the backbone of the Christian way of life that we teach. Catechesis must, then, pay great attention to how we live out our faith in the marketplace and at home, and pay great attention to how we are called to love our neighbor in word and in deed and by costly example every day. This is where the sharpness of the cutting edge can be felt: in the mission, in the willingness, however clumsy or tentative, to be the means by which God's love abounds in the world. And these are, therefore, some of the clues we look for to tell us that the catechumens are ready to become "the elect." We need to taste their salt and see their light shining—not in the church but against the darkness of the night outside. The elect are the sign that God still refuses to give up on the world; indeed they are coming to participate in God's reign, inaugurated by Christ. They are the means by which God continues to make his presence known, a presence that calls all people into a new life. If these words are not to be empty rhetoric, the church must always seek the meaning of its election in the context of its mission.

The ultimate resolution that the Christian tradition finds to the problem of the nations set up by the Tower of Babel is, of course, Pentecost—through the outpouring of the Spirit, people of every nation hear the good news in their own languages and become one in love and gratitude to God. To the extent that the catechumenate—especially in a diocesan setting—involves bringing together in faith people of different languages and cultures and all strata of society, the church is in a privileged position for realizing this good news in both a symbolic and a real way, and should know it. The people themselves are the most powerful symbol in the Rite of Election. The church's choice of them and their assent—in all the ways in which these things are realized in the rite—is the working out of God's will. We do well to respect the scale of this undertaking. God's will is worked out on many planes: by the **53** sanctification of individuals, by the collective witness of the church to this work of the Spirit, by the progress of the mission entrusted to the church by Christ and by the reconciliation of peoples with God and with one another. Election is big enough to embrace all of these things. Indeed, it should recall all of them to us as we stand on the threshold of Lent together.

Some will say that the stories of primordial evil and its catastrophic consequences in Genesis, and the evocation of judgment involved in New Testament eschatology, make too gloomy an impression on people today. These stories take such a dark view—sin emerges again and again, and God's judgment is fearsome—that they appear to speak to us from a past and about a future that seem far away from our comfortable and enlightened present. "People are basically good," the common wisdom goes; is it necessary to depict them as being in such dire straits? This is an important question, and an inevitable one in our society, which is generally optimistic about human nature.

Is the human race in dire straits or not? Perhaps each person must finally answer that question individually. But the Christian tradition has always held that the answer is yes, that it is not a question of wanting but of *needing* salvation, that God's grace pulls us out of despair, back from the brink of chaos and into a hope that we could not otherwise dare to hope. The world that practices all kinds of sin and cruelty and is subjected to the evils of suffering and death is the very world into which God "gave his only Son, so that whoever believes in him may not die but may have eternal life" (John 3:16). Into this world God sent his Son out of love. The catechumens and candidates themselves bear the scars of living in such a world as well as the promise of new life that is God's sure gift to them. And those who believe in Christ are continually sent into the world to be light, salt and leaven until he comes again.

Election does not take place in a safe environment, as a kind of badge of special honor placed on a few lucky, chosen ones among others who are merely not so well favored. Election is about what God is doing in answer to a desperate situation brought on by sin in all its forms. Election is about the salvation brought about by Christ in a way that is cosmic, communal and—not least of all—personal. Election is about a God who leans toward humanity in spite of everything, a God whose love will not let us go.

Is the Rite of Election about Election?

Some may wish to object that while the theology of election is all very well and good, in fact it has very little to do with the liturgical rite in question. Isn't the Rite of Election about the choices made by the church? And are we not justified therefore in regarding this rite simply and solely as the church's choosing of certain people to whom the sacraments will be given? In other words, some may wish to argue that the meaning of the Rite of Election is rooted in human community and that the doctrine of election is a piece of excess theological baggage.

To address this objection, we must look again at the historical roots of the rite. Some of the Latin-speaking churches in ancient times called the candidates for the Easter sacraments "the elect" *(electi),* the chosen, from the time of the rite in which their names were enrolled. The scriptural background of the word election was certainly known to the church in that period. The notion that the ancient church knew about the biblical language of election and prominently used the word "elect" in one of its initiatory rites but did not intend to make a connection between these two things is extremely implausible.

The ancient church was highly conscious of symbol. The religious language of its rites was soaked through with scriptural imagery. It would be absurd to think that, for instance, the crossing of the Red Sea could be used as a type for baptism but that "the elect" going through these waters

55

would fail to suggest that they are "the chosen people" by divine election. It is inconceivable that the New Testament could often call the church "the elect" and that those who are becoming members of the ancient church could be named "the elect" at a critical juncture of the catechumenate merely by coincidence. In the same way, it would be foolish to think that the terms *illuminandi* and *photizomenoi* ("those being enlightened") made reference merely to the mental processes of the catechumens and not to "Christ the light of the world." In all these instances *(electi, illuminandi* and *photizomenoi)*, the presumed subject is not the human community, but God himself. The elect are chosen by God; the illuminated are illuminated by God; the enlightened are enlightened by God.[34]

It is true that there were other churches, both Latin- and Greek-speaking, that called the candidates for baptism something other than "elect." But we are initially prompted today to give special attention to the name "elect" because our modern rite gives preference to the name "elect." The candidates are always called "the elect," and the rite is named first of all "election." Other names are only mentioned in passing. Had preference been given to *photizomenoi* or *illuminandi* in the modern rite, perhaps we would be justified in seeking out scriptural and theological sources that would enlarge our appreciation of what being "enlightened by Christ" means. Even so, the other symbolic texts of the ancient rite as we know them and as they have been preserved in the modern rite—testimony and judgment, choosing, inscription of names, the book—all point directly not to scriptures about enlightenment but to scriptural texts dealing with election. Testimony and judgment by the church recalls the final judgment at which the elect will be vindicated. Choosing by the bishop recalls the actions of the apostles, under the guidance of the Holy Spirit, that were so important to the founding of the church. Inscription of names and the book recall the book of life. These symbolic words, actions and objects all point to election.

Even if the people who participated in this rite were called something else, the rite would still be about divine election. The theology of election is not extra baggage for the Rite of Election to carry: it is the engine that drives it.

We do well to remember that in the ancient church, there was no dichotomy between the church's sacramental business and the eternal horizon of its faith. The sacramental business was regarded as the work of God, not secondarily but primarily. Modern people may be prone to reduce religious rites to exercises of human community, but the ancient churches from which the rites of the catechumenate spring did not suffer from this problem. Modern documents of the liturgy continue to stress that our rites are the work of God in Christ. These rites are about the interactions of the human community of the church only insofar as this church is essentially constituted by and sustained by God's activity.

The Rite of Election does not claim that God's election is limited by what goes on in our liturgical celebration of election. (God certainly may choose more people than turn up at the Rite of Election!) Nor even is the mystery of divine election in the church exhaustively celebrated by the rite. Baptism itself is the epicenter of the church's celebration of divine election; the Rite of Election calls the elect forward to that sacrament of regeneration. But there is no reason for declaring that those who come through this rite are "the elect," apart from the conviction that God has chosen them and destined them for eternal life—the life that will be given to them in the sacraments of initiation.

In sum, we cannot afford to let divine election slip into the background in order to concentrate on the fact that what is transpiring is also a limited, human event, or even a churchly event. To do so would be to sell out the theology and symbolism of the rite, and remarkably cheaply at that. Certainly the Rite of Election is about choosing people for the sacraments. But to assert this only begs the question: Whose work are the sacraments? They are God's work, clearly, or the church is in deep trouble. What are the sacraments of initiation if not the means by which the elect enter into their inheritance, the reign of God? The celebrant of the Rite of Election is enjoined in paragraph 125 to "open to all the divine mystery" that is at hand in the election of these catechumens, for it is a *divine* mystery that is taking place in the church. This "divine mystery" deserves no less than first claim on the attention of those who celebrate the rite.

Chapter 4

Meet the Bishop

■

American culture is traditionally suspicious of authority and wary of the power of office. After all, a crucial aspect of America's "break from the past" was the rejection of royalty and all that it entailed: no hereditary thrones for us, and no aristocracy either. Naturally, no society can get along without any authority or office at all—order and the smooth functioning of society demand it. But we prefer to play these things down. One result of this little tension between necessity and self-image is that we feel better when people in authority and holders of office demonstrate that they are, after all, "just folks."

Americans look for personal charisma and personal achievement in their leaders, not symbolic significance and hierarchically based power. The one symbolic function that the American leader must typically serve is to appear democratic—that is to say, friendly to all and down-to-earth. In other words, the successful American leader must confirm the American cultural myth that we are all on **59** equal footing; authority and office really do not matter. In fact, the more that the reality of the power of office and authority press themselves on our consciousness, the greater the relief and pleasure of discovering that people in such positions are in fact not very different from ourselves. That these discoveries are generally quite well rehearsed and are managed by public relations specialists does not diminish their effectiveness; we want to be sold. We believe in our cultural mythology.

American political leaders have found it to their advantage to present an image that stresses the personal. Candidates do not win elections by discussing political issues but by projecting a persona that the people feel they can trust. We are living in the age of the celebrity, in which the canons of the entertainment world, through the mass media, have gained ascendancy in the political realm. These canons always guide us back to what is familiar ground: the personal. The American public has a boundless appetite for the personal from public figures, not only in the form of scandal but also in the details of life: likes and dislikes, what one eats for breakfast, house pets. Reassuring and undemanding, these details confirm us in what we want to believe: that leadership does not call for sacrifice and loyalty from the led but merely camaraderie and trust. We look to the personal to redeem the political from its uncomfortable associations with the real power of office and the demands generated by the exercise of authority.

The problem with all this lies not in the fact that office and authority need to be redeemed, for they certainly do. They contain the potential for evil as well as for good, and always have. There are sound reasons why Americans have ambivalent feelings about authority and office, and why presidents, chairpersons and other leaders all bear watching, lest their exercise of power fail to promote the common good. The glaring error here is, rather, that we put such implicit confidence in the personal to redeem the political. This it cannot do, and the attempt to pretend otherwise has aided the decline of American public life. The personal is a shortcut to nowhere, a placebo for a real problem, an answer that is no answer because it merely changes the question. The political can only be redeemed by the worthiness of a community's reasons for existing and by the service of the leaders and the led to worthy objectives, not by assuring ourselves that our leaders are likable people.

Why do so many people want to shake the bishop's hand in the Rite of Election? Why is it such a thrill to "meet the bishop" that it becomes for many the centerpiece of their experience of the rite? Why would so many veteran catechumenate ministers prefer to do without the "hoopla" surrounding the bishop? Why do so many of the same ministers grudgingly admit that "the people love it, though"? One answer is surely that divine election is not well understood, the special qualities of the Rite of Election are not well appreciated, and therefore other things have rushed in to fill the vacuum. But the pleasure taken in the discovery of the personal warmth of the bishop's greeting cannot be accounted for by this answer alone. A hunger is being fed by the "hoopla" around the bishop, and one must ask, what is this hunger?

It would be exceedingly naive to assume that catechumens and candidates—any more than the Catholics who populate our American parishes—do not have profound ambivalence about authority in the church. We may cheer for this or that pastoral letter of the bishops, or we may support one or another stand of the hierarchy; but as democratic Americans we are deeply uncomfortable with anything that stands over our freedom as individuals and presumes to make a claim on us.

Bishops stand at the nerve center of this ambivalence. It would be foolish to think otherwise or to imagine that the attitudes we bring to episcopal events are unrelated to this ambivalence. The parish may descend into the cultural mire of viewing itself as a spiritual service center, parish priests may adopt a preaching style that is fairly indistinguishable from the patter of religious talk-show hosts, but where you have a bishop, you have hierarchy; there is no getting around it. And we have mixed feelings about hierarchy; respect for office does not go without saying, but suspicion of office does. Some people undoubtedly come to grips with authority in the church, theologically and personally, but this is comparatively rare. Most people have a tentative synthesis of beliefs, mental habits and emotional trip wires that enable them to—sort of—accept authority without relinquishing our cultural mythology, such as it is.

The popularity of the handshake of the bishop as the crucial ritual action of the Rite of Election is a triumph of American cultural mythology. It attempts to redeem the political with the personal. The personal touch feeds our hunger to be loved; it gives momentary relief to our anxieties about authority; it reassures us—American style— that hierarchs are really "just folks"; and it has nothing to do with election. It proceeds from the mistaken premise that the Rite of Election is about the bishop and goes on to turn this encounter from an anxious one into a happy one. That it is successful distracts us from the fact that in order to attend to this agenda we have had to abandon the agenda of the rite itself.

The Bishop's Welcome

The sincere but confused nature of the pleas that have been made in support of this practice illustrate the irrelevance of this gesture to election. "It means so much to them. . . . It's the only time that they [the catechumens and candidates] will ever meet with him [the bishop] and experience his warmth as a human being." If this is true, if the bishop is really so distant a character from the ongoing pastoral ministry of the church, it shows why people hunger so much for personal contact with him. But it is all the more reason not to ritualize a friendliness that has no prospect of being realized beyond the rite. The argument unwittingly assigns the handshake/welcome a compensatory function that speaks exceedingly ill of the normal standard of community life in the church. Where the bishop does exercise a pastoral presence, no ritual handshakes are necessary; where he does not, no handshakes can possibly make up for it.

On the general rationale for including the handshake in the center of the rite, one hears, "That's what we're all about: welcome!" Within this comment one hears the understandable longing for a warmer and more welcoming church as well as the mistake of taking one aspect of initiation and subordinating all other aspects to it. For some Catholics, the church has been at times a very cold and unsympathetic place, and the discovery of personal warmth in church community is *the* liberating discovery of their lives. *Welcome* is the code word for everything loving and kind about the church. The problem with this is not that one wishes for a cold and forbidding church, but that *welcome*—even as it is used by its most enthusiastic advocates—is not a big enough concept to embrace everything that is meant by *conversion,* which is in fact "what we are all about." Furthermore, the Rite of Election is not a rite of welcome; and as one astute observer put it, "the bishop is not a minister of hospitality."

On the question of whether shaking the bishop's hand after the service might be sufficient, the argument is sometimes advanced: "Our bishop is not very personable; he does better with something that is actually programmed in the liturgy." Here again the ritual is being made to serve a compensatory function and is further subordinated to the task of compensating for the idiosyncrasies of the bishop himself! The goal of a personal encounter with a personable bishop is presumed to be of sufficient importance that it can be allowed to organize the rest of the event around itself. There is no question that when the bishop does greet each catechumen and candidate, the action dominates the event. **63**

Even the most perfunctory handshake takes time—an inordinate amount of time when there are many catechumens and candidates. But the question remains: Can the other elements of the rite afford to take a back seat without robbing the rite of its essential meaning?

The rite itself does allow for a certain amount of attention to be given to the individual candidates by the bishop wherever possible, without that attention being a "personal encounter" where the personability or human warmth of the bishop is at issue. The candidates are called before the bishop by name, personal testimony concerning them is delivered in his hearing, and each one's name is enrolled in his presence. These are kindly forms by which the interchange between bishop and candidates advances the purposes of the rite. All of these interactions are to the point; it is clear that the candidates—not the bishop—are the focus of the event. In all of them it is clear that what is happening to the candidates by God's grace—not by this close encounter with the episcopacy—is the focus of this event. The presentation, the testimony and the enrollment are all parts of one reality that is being worked out by the church through the ministry of the godparents and the assembly and under the pastoral presidency of its bishop.

Ironically, the "welcoming" handshake by the bishop inserted into this concerted effort throws a wrench into the works because it invariably shifts attention away from the candidates, the godparents, the testimony and the enrollment and onto the bishop himself. The Rite of Election is not about the bishop, but it is hard to tell this when the main action of the liturgy becomes the ritual of shaking his hand.

This "adaptation" of the Rite of Election also easily begins to resemble countless other nonliturgical events where people want to meet the bishop and where his cordiality is gratefully received: picture-taking after confirmation, communion breakfasts for church societies and charitable groups, anniversary celebrations for married couples and so on. Everyone wants to meet the bishop, and he is typically the center of a great deal of attention. The elect may be thrilled to meet the bishop at the moment in which this occurs in the Rite of Election, but eventually they will find out that the bishop does the same routine with countless other people in countless other circumstances much more trivial than that of their election. The episcopal receiving line is only too common. But normally this activity is not thought important enough theologically to go on within the rites of the church; it happens outside of them. Why in the order of Christian initiation of adults should our practice be any different?

One must ask the question: Does not this importation into the Rite of Election—for nowhere does the rite suggest that the bishop welcome the candidates in this way—hinder and confuse the purposes of the rite itself? A legitimate adaptation furthers the genuine purposes of a rite; any adaptation, however enjoyable, must be measured against the criteria of the rite's own inherent meaning and direction. The confusion the handshake causes in the Rite of Election would be reason enough to disqualify it as a legitimate adaptation. It also seems to duplicate the welcoming function of the Rite of Acceptance and Welcome, and it improperly anticipates the Easter Vigil kiss of peace that traditionally follows the consignation after baptism.

The Bishop's Leadership

When the church gathers for the Rite of Election, there are plenty of tokens of the office and authority of the bishop in evidence. We cannot get around them; nor should we. Miter, crozier, cathedra and pectoral cross, however resolutely ignored, will speak for themselves. It is best that they do not say that these are "trappings" beneath which a likable personality attracts us, that these are forbidding tokens of an unpalatable authoritarianism or that these are prized possessions of self-satisfied men, but that these are symbols of Christ, who rules and shepherds and presides over his church. But there is no brief or didactic way to communicate this message; it is either conveyed by the whole community of the church as its deeply held tradition—and reinforced by the quality of the bishop's preaching and teaching, pastoring and presiding—or not at all.

The political in the church, as well as outside of it, is redeemed not by the personal but by the worthiness of the reasons for the existence of the community itself and by leaders' service of worthy objectives within it. Leaders who serve worthy objectives, who understand the reasons for the community's life and advance them, will always command respect, countervailing cultural attitudes notwithstanding. If, on the contrary, the reasons for the existence of the church are lost in the mists of history, or if leaders are doing something other than serving objectives that are worthy, then personal warmth and welcome will put off only briefly the day of judgment.

By the orthodoxy of their teaching, their faithfulness to the liturgy and their assiduous shepherding of their people, bishops are symbols of the unity of the church. The unity they symbolize is that which is hard-won by the blood of Christ, not a friendliness that is here today and gone tomorrow. Their office is also symbolic in that they are expected to point us to Christ, who is not "just folks" but is himself our Teacher, High Priest and Shepherd.

Bishops are expected to exercise a special responsibility for the initiation of adults. Why? Perhaps because they are expected to know best how to animate the church for its mission, which is at the heart of adult conversion and believing. The unexpected resolution of the subterranean anxieties about hierarchy, authority and office lie not in the bishop being a great guy to whom we can all relate but in his making a concerted effort with others to attend to the business of the rite: the election by which God takes us from being "no people" and makes us into "God's people" (1 Peter 2:10).

In the election of catechumens, the church collectively—godparents, catechumens and the assembly—brings to a pass the fulfillment of (dare we say it?) God's sovereign will. What goes on in election is not a welcoming but a turning point for the elect: the hinge, the pivot, the "Yes" that precipitates the consummation of the whole process of initiation. It is a liturgy so important that the bishop himself presides over it and helps us see through it to the mission that election serves.

Chapter 5

Welcome to the Larger Church

■

Despite the fact that we Catholics traditionally prize the heritage of a worldwide church—a church much larger than the parish—we tend not to think too much about the diocese as a locus of affection or a source of pride and ecclesial identity. The center of Catholic church life in the United States is in the parishes, and it takes some doing to pry us out of them to go to the cathedral, even for special occasions. Unless the cathedral is one's parish, one generally feels like a visitor there, rarely at home. Many dioceses are far-flung, and trips to the cathedral can be time-consuming and difficult.

Prior to the reform of the initiation of adults, the cathedral had not been the conspicuous center for the church's initiatory rites. Ordinations, the Chrism Mass and special Masses for select groups were more in the cathedral's line. The initiatory sacraments certainly were celebrated there as elsewhere, but the elsewhere predominated in the popular mind. Even confirmations, at which the bishop ordinarily presides, have been long associated not with visits to the cathedral but with the bishop's pastoral visits to the parishes.

The Cathedral as Setting for Election

Establishing the practice of having all parish catechumenate groups attend the Rite of Election in a cathedral setting has been a real accomplishment. The general difficulty of realizing a directive that requires parish groups to do something new, such as have a celebration in a diocesan setting, has been compounded by the early successes of the catechumenate in the womb of the parish. The ministers of the catechumenate at the parish level have tended therefore to be a bit jealous of their prerogatives and somewhat reluctant to let the child wander from home for any of its rites. Hence, even for those amenable to travel to the cathedral, the first forays into diocesan liturgy tended to be not at a diocesan Rite of Election but at optional occasions after inititation, such as Masses for the neophytes. Yet the document clearly directs that the Rite of Election should be a diocesan liturgy. The *praenotanda* indicate not only that the bishop or his delegate is its usual presider (RCIA, #121) but that the cathedral is its normal setting (RCIA, #127). To accommodate the high degree of ownership and interest in this rite on the parish level, however, the parish Rite of Sending was devised as one of the adaptations made available in 1988 for the dioceses of the United States.

The Rite of Sending and the Rite of Election have enjoyed a symbiotic relationship. Though optional, the Rite of Sending is almost always done in the parish when election is celebrated at the cathedral. The business of election, once accomplished in one rite, now is spread out over two. The presentation of catechumens, with the calling of individual names, can be done in both settings but is frequently more fully celebrated in the parish Rite of Sending. The testimony of godparents is included in both rites, but it is frequently more elaborate and personal in the parish Rite of Sending. The signing of the Book of the Elect may occur in either rite, but frequently it is assigned to the parish Rite of Sending.

Election, for its part, always has a presentation of catechumens and the testimony of godparents. And Election alone has the assent of the catechumens themselves and the bishop's act of election. The actual enrollment of names, even if the book is signed at the Rite of Sending, always takes place at the Rite of Election. If done properly, the balance favors Election; that is to say, the content of the Rite of Election is a complete statement in itself and is not diminished by the way that parts of the election are anticipated in the Rite of Sending. But the undertow, because of the general tendencies outlined above, pulls in the direction of the parish, not the diocese.

Not surprisingly, people have found much to like in the cathedral celebrations of the rite. The setting itself lends a particular power to the occasion. Having experienced this rite at the cathedral, people understand that the bishop has an integral part in initiation and that the cathedral is indeed a conspicuous center for at least some of the rites of initiation. It is deeply traditional, and it makes sense within the structure of the local (diocesan) church that some of the key events that propel our common life forward should happen in the cathedral or, at least, in some place where the local church can gather.

But at times the setting for the rite has assumed a greater role than it should in determining in people's minds what exactly Election is about. The setting is not the *raison d'être* of the rite, but it is sometimes proposed as such. Why do we have a Rite of Election that is, by definition, a diocesan rite? For many, the answer seems self-evident: to give the catechumens "a sense of the larger church." The Rite of Election has commonly been viewed as a ceremony of welcome to the diocesan church. It is difficult to overestimate the currency of this perception; it is ubiquitous. **71**

This idea accords well with the notion that the centerpiece of the rite is the act of meeting the bishop, which was discussed in the previous chapter. But while it enjoys a certain plausibility because the elect and the candidates do come away with a new appreciation of the diocesan church after having experienced the diocesan Rite of Election, it has no basis in the rite itself nor in the traditions from which the rite springs.

When the question of "why go to a diocesan Rite of Election?" was first posed in the context of seeking a change away from election in the parish, the answer necessarily emphasized the value of gathering with the larger church. It was presumed (too sanguinely, perhaps) that everyone knew what election was; what needed to be communicated were the peculiar benefits that the diocesan celebration supplied over and above what could be had when the rite was celebrated in the parish. The present situation is a continuation of this trend. A reorganization of ideas can happen when the Rite of Sending takes into itself many of the salient features of election and yet is not election: Sending carries quite a bit of the meaning of election, and Election is made to carry only the remainder— the diocesan part. As such, it easily falls into being seen as a rite of welcome into the larger church. This construction, however, is not at all sufficient for understanding election. And it is also problematic to underplay what happens at the parish by calling it *sending* if, in fact, it is the very stuff of election.

The document itself is unselfconscious about the diocesan setting in which it places the rite. The setting does not provide the rationale for the rite; it is the logical consequence of following certain principles, such as historical continuity with liturgical traditions and faithfulness to a specifically Catholic ecclesiology and church structure. The *praenotanda* of the Rite of Election are unimpressed by the catechetical value of the diocesan setting and beauty of the cathedral. The idea of awing anyone with the size of the diocese or the number of elect, if it ever occurred to the framers of the modern rite, is never hinted at in print, either in the drafts of the document, the reports of the *coetus* or the summary statements of what was learned by the field tests of the various drafts of the document. And the notion of being welcomed into another community on the occasion of election is totally foreign to the rite.

The Problems of *Welcome*

The *praenotanda* give substantial indications of what the Rite of Election is about: discernment, the church's choosing, God's choosing, the testimony of godparents, the assent of the elect, the enrollment of names and the commencement of the lenten retreat. There is no lack of content in the Rite of Election. The dignified existence of a diocesan church is presumed, but it is not in any way the subject of the rite.

As members of their parishes, catechumens are already considered to belong to their diocese—so much so that they are entitled to transact the important business of their election in the midst of the assembled local church. To welcome them at this point is to place them again at the door when they have been well past that threshold for some time.

We have already identified the problem of taking the legitimate theme of "welcome" in the catechumenate and subordinating other equally important or more important aspects of the ritual repertoire of Christian initiation to this one theme. On the surface, the hegemony of hospitality may seem to be a benign thing, for who can find fault with welcome? Welcome is an ever-popular and attractive offer to members of our increasingly deracinated and insecure society. Whether it be welcome to the parish or welcome to the diocesan church, welcome provides something that people want and need. Furthermore, people who are in transition, such as catechumens and candidates, are by definition insecure. What could possibly be wrong with surrounding them with welcome every step of the way? Isn't the point of all the activity of Christian initiation to welcome people into the church?

There are two fundamental problems with the "welcome" rationale for the Rite of Election, beyond its redundancy with the welcoming function of the Rite of Acceptance into the Order of Catechumens. First, anything that takes our attention away from the business proper to the rite, however well intentioned, is a distraction that causes other material of value to be de-emphasized or lost. Distortion of the proper emphases of the rituals of Christian initiation ultimately is not a benign phenomenon but a subversive one. In this case, it subverts by weakening. If our minds and hearts are predisposed to regard the purpose of election as providing a welcome to the larger church, we will not be able to attend equally well to the themes of decision and commitment, which are so plainly intended to be the center of the Rite of Election and in which the rite's real power resides.

Our experience of religious ritual is rich and complex and it cannot be reduced to one narrow meaning. But each of the rites of initiation has a kind of internal logic that gives it a particular shape or direction that enables it to hold many meanings but still remain identifiably what it is. A liturgy of election that is substantially about election is not thereby prevented from being an occasion of human warmth or of the genuine exuberance of a powerful, large-group liturgy. It does not exclude its participants from awe at being in a beautiful cathedral or from exhilaration at being among hundreds of people who are enthusiastic about joining the church. Rather, it grounds all of these phenomena in what is the essential meaning and direction of the rite, and it organizes the peripheral around what is essential.

Interestingly enough, a rite that has as its principal message "welcome to the larger church" is very tame in comparison to a rite that exults in a divine decision for humanity that has the power to change both us and the world. When election is done well, we see people spontaneously cheering and reveling in the events that take place in that rite. No one could possibly get so excited about being welcomed to the diocesan church, nor should they. The source of this enthusiasm is, rather, in what God is doing in and through these people whom the church calls elect. It is marvelous, it is a mighty deed, it gets people up on their feet, and it is worth cheering about.

Second, a Christian theological perspective imposes, or should impose, a healthy critical distance from the notion that initiation is chiefly about the surface phenomena of warm handshakes and all the cheerfully indiscriminate gestures of acceptance that people normally associate with the word *welcome*. Such a theological perspective gives a deeper dimension to our understanding of what the journey of conversion involves. The one unfortunate and unintended side effect of the otherwise fruitful metaphor of the "journey" for initiation is that it can be misinterpreted in an excessively linear fashion; initiation then is regarded as something like a sight-seeing tour, where it is enough to express interest and appreciation of a lovely view before one's attention is directed to a new scene. When the initiation journey is thus understood, interior change is not essential to the exercises of catechesis and the liturgies in question. Initiation, as it is rightly understood in the order of Christian initiation and in the tradition of the church, however, involves a progressive deepening of conversion within the context of sin and grace. It produces important interior changes. Each successive station on the journey should be understood not just as a new environment but as an occasion for marking a new depth within the person as well.

People certainly have a need for hospitality when they arrive at an unfamiliar place. Insofar as *welcome* denotes basic hospitality, there can be no quarrel with it. There is nothing wrong with greeting people warmly, helping them find their way, attending to their needs and so on. These simple kindnesses require a certain amount of forethought if they are to be administered to, say, 2,000 people in a setting where very few of them are truly "at home." To say that election is not a rite of welcome is not to minimize the importance of hospitality whenever the church gathers, especially when it gathers in unfamiliar surroundings. It is, rather, to hold out for something more important as the meaning of the Rite of Election—namely, that it is a crucial turning point in the deepening conversion of the elect, leading them to the Easter Vigil.

The dismissal that ends the Rite of Election recalls that the next meeting will be at the Scrutiny. This seems to be an exceedingly odd way to end a ceremony orchestrated for the purpose of welcoming people to the larger church: "Welcome!—and, by the way, we'll next see you at your solemn exorcism." But if election is the turning point, the decisive moment when God, the church and the person experiencing conversion say, "Yes, we are going through with this," then it is not so strange to reconvene at a solemn exorcism.[1] To do so is merely to go through with it, as we have promised to do.

Election is not a rite of welcome, but it does hold an invitation. The Rite of Election is an invitation into the desert of Lent, with Jesus Christ and with the whole church, there to find or rediscover the meaning of one's call for the life of the world. Election takes us to the next step; it invites the elect forward into the period of purification and enlightenment.

Chapter 6

Who Signs the Book?

■

One of the most important tasks of the committee that drafted the American adaptations of the *Rite of Christian Initiation of Adults* was to produce adaptations of the rites for the baptized while still maintaining enough distinctive material for catechumens that the primacy of part I of the rite would not be obscured. Maintaining a visible distinction between the unbaptized catechumen and the baptized candidate has been held to be of crucial importance. There are several reasons for this.

First of all, the reform of the rites of initiation of adults is primarily a reform of the baptismal polity of the church. The rite articulates a renewed vision of baptism. Once one grasps that vision, a renewed understanding of many other aspects of the church's life follows, and various other manifestations of initiation fall into their proper places. But one only comes to such integration and renewal by understanding what the reform of baptism means. A lot rides on whether or not the people of the church "get it" concerning baptism, and in order to get it they have to see it in all the rites of the catechumenate, not just in the rite of baptism itself.

Second, ecumenical sensitivity demands that the church visibly respect the valid baptism of non-Catholic Christians, who are already members of Christ's body, no matter how uncatechized they may be. In a similar way, as long as the church continues to make the claims it does about the objective efficacy of infant baptism, the sacramental status of baptized Catholics must be honored, even though subjectively these candidates may be thoroughly comparable to the catechumens. Just a short slide down the slippery slope from confusing the baptized candidates with the catechumens lies the "pastoral use" of rebaptism, a practice followed by some Protestant denominations and advocated by some Catholics. The Catholic church officially rejects it, however, as alien to its view of what baptism is and does.

Yet the prospect of having the catechumens and the baptized candidates completely separated would not be ideal. It is appropriate that their formation be shared in common, because the catechetical needs of both groups are often so similar. Participation in the rites of the catechumenate by the baptized has been shown to have great pastoral value for the candidates themselves, and it gives a coherence to their formation that would otherwise be lacking. The order allows for baptized but uncatechized adults to take part in the process and in the rites in some fitting way, though it does not specify what this way looks like. Therefore, the challenge of constructing parallel or combined rites that include the baptized is a worthwhile and important project. It is, however, fraught with conflicts because the desire to include the baptized in the rites with the catechumens inevitably clashes with the strategic imperative to maintain visible distinctions between the two groups.

Do the Candidates Sign the Book?

The decisions about the combined rites for catechumens and baptized candidates for the American adaptations of the RCIA are therefore some of the most difficult and delicate that had to be made. The decisions reached run the gamut from a willingness to include the two groups together with little more than verbal distinctions in how they are addressed (as in the Rite of Acceptance) to the demand that the two be separated completely (as in the Scrutinies). In the case of the Rite of Election, the American committee that devised the combined rite confined the signing of the Book of the Elect to the elect alone, excluding the baptized candidates from this gesture but not from the rite itself—which is known as the Rite of Election and Call to Continuing Conversion when the baptized candidates are included in it. This decision has been put into practice, but not without protest and a little cheating here and there (e.g., "Our catechumens sign the Book of the Elect. Our candidates sign a scroll.").

Some of the protest has taken the form of sponsors and candidates feeling aggrieved because the candidates were excluded from part of the rite. In other words, the principle that there should be distinctions either was not understood or was not accepted. People certainly were not well prepared for this decision if their parish catechumenates mixed the two groups indiscriminately or if they had been influenced by the practice of devising paraliturgies of enrollment for confirmation candidates in which all the young candidates sign a book and receive some kind of encouragement for their efforts. But in addition to the protest against distinctions on principle, there has been protest based on the rite as well.

The two sides of the controversy concerning who signs the book can be summarized briefly. One side holds that the signing of the book is a symbol of the person's assent and commitment[1] to go forward to the completion of initiation at

Easter, and so both groups should sign. The other side argues that the signing of the book is enrollment preparatory to baptism and so is unnecessary for the candidates, who by virtue of their baptism are already as "signed up" and enrolled as they will ever need to be.

Invocation of the biblical image of the "book of life" has sometimes been used to emphasize the once-in-a-lifetime nature of enrollment, associating the signing more closely with baptism and therefore weighing in on the side of limiting the signing to those who will be baptized. The "book of life" image could as easily be used in support of the other side of the controversy, however, if one recalls that one's name *can* be blotted out of the book of life (Exodus 32:32, 33; Psalm 69:28) and therefore might need to be rewritten.[2] Also, having one's name "written in heaven" (Luke 10:20) is closely associated with discipleship (Philippians 4:3) and is therefore associated with what the catechumens and candidates hold in common rather than with what distinguishes them.

The image of the book of life is closely associated with election in the New Testament and has a strong eschatological flavor.[3] It appears in the Old Testament, too, in conjunction with election and predestination.[4] St. Augustine describes the book of life as a tool of the final judgment, a book in which all the good and evil deeds that people do are recorded[5] along with their names. Thus St. Thomas Aquinas was able to spin out the metaphor of the book as the way that God keeps firmly in mind the elect themselves, all that God has done for them (the scriptures)[6] and all that God still is doing for them to bring them to glory (the good that God gives them the grace to do).[7] The book of life was a favorite image of Martin Luther,[8] who regarded Christ himself as the book of life[9] in which alone the believer may read assurance of his or her election (Calvin preferred to call Christ the *speculum electionis,* or mirror of election).[10] There are obvious affinities between the symbolism of our liturgical book and the eschatological book; it is therefore an appealing idea to use the "book of life" texts when talking about the Book of the Elect.

It must be noted, however, that our Book of the Elect is not exactly the book of life. Though we may nourish our imagination on biblical texts concerning the latter, the former is related to a concrete liturgical history, which makes it quite a bit more specific than the book of life that appears in the biblical texts. The book of life exists in the mind of God; the Book of the Elect exists on a shelf in the catechumenate director's office. The most obvious difference in their contents, other than the fact that the Almighty can be presumed to keep better records than we do, is that, as we saw in chapter 1, some of the ancient sources record that the godparents' names were entered into the book along with the names of the elect—a practice that the modern rite quietly preserves as one of its options. The idea of having the godparents sign as surety for the catechumens they present to the bishop casts a different light on the book: The book may serve not only as a record of who is called to the new life of baptism but may serve also as a means of holding the godparents responsible for the elect.

Some may say that this argues on the side of having the baptized candidates sign, because once it is clear that non-catechumens (i.e., the godparents) are signing the book, we have broken the rule that baptized persons do not sign. Also, the weight of symbolism is again thrown on the side of the book as a document of commitment rather than a record of sacramental status. On the other hand, one is obliged to note that godparents and candidates are in totally different categories, despite the fact that both are baptized; one cannot infer the inclusion of one because of the inclusion of the other. Furthermore, the ancient sources cannot be used to argue against the Book of the Elect as uniquely oriented toward baptism, however much commitment is symbolized, because the class of persons known to us as "candidates" was simply unknown to the ancient church. Candidates are a later development.

The decision of the American drafting committee seems, on balance, to have been a good one. If the signing had not been reserved for the catechumens, it is hard to imagine what other part of the rite might have been held as unique to them. Verbal distinctions (for instance, between the bishop's "act of election" and his "call to conversion") are the weakest of distinctions; the fact that only the catechumens are enrolled in the book is a much more effective demonstration that the groups are different.

Does the Bishop Sign the Book?

During the same period that restrictions on the candidates' signing were being put into practice, another signer of the book emerged in some places. Having the bishop sign the Book of the Elect during the rite is a development that never appeared in any of the ancient traditions pertaining to this ritual. Nor did it appear in the experimental versions of the modern rite, in its final draft or in any of its American adaptations, but it has cropped up in practice in some American dioceses. The rationale for the practice is that by signing the book the bishop is "ratifying" the act of the catechumens' signing.

Outside of the fact that this practice is a modern innovation that has no basis at all in church tradition—a serious objection in itself—there are other reasons against it as well. First of all, it violates the symbolism of the signing. The inscription of names of the elect is a symbol of their commitment and is their enrollment for baptism. They are not signing a contract to which there are several parties. They are not signing a bill into law or establishing a legislative decision that must be ratified by the bishop. They are entering their names in a roll, such as one might do in a roster for military conscription—an analogy frequently used in the ancient church to explain the enrollment of names. Their giving of their names is the focus of the signing. The bishop does not sign his name in the book in this rite because he is not the one being initiated. Neither is he standing as surety for the catechumens, as the godparents are. The bishop's commitment is simply not at issue in this part of the rite.

Second, having the bishop sign, especially if the elect have signed at the parish and the bishop alone signs in the cathedral, places too much emphasis on the bishop. The focus of the signing in the rite should be on the elect. Like the personal greeting by the bishop, the signing of each Book of the Elect by the bishop takes time and draws the assembly's attention to him and what he does at a point when he is not supposed to be the focus of attention.

Third, introducing a ceremonial signing by the bishop confuses the two different functions of the book. The Book of the Elect is both a ceremonial book and a record book. The publishers of books for this dual purpose do in fact provide a space for the name of the bishop. This line assists in the legitimate function of the book as a record of the event of the catechumens' election. The name of the presiding bishop may be entered into that space at any time and by anyone. The fact that there is a space available in the book for it does not make entering the bishop's name a suitable liturgical action any more than a line for the date would render suitable a ceremonial reckoning of the month and day of the year.

What's in a Name?

A person's name is the most important symbol of who that person is. All the business concerning names in the rite is grounded in this fundamental fact. A name possesses the marvelous qualities that all words do: Spoken, it is an event in the present moment; written, it perdures through time; heard, it conveys a message. Your name is the word by which you are known. People are the only creatures who have names and give names; it marks us as the human race. A name expresses individuality, but also family and clan, bonds and commitments, blood ties and birthrights. To know the name of God was the unparalleled privilege of the chosen people; to be called by name by this God, the height of human felicity. To be forced to take on a strange name, as in the case of slavery, is an oppression; to be known by one's own true name, a liberation. The citizens of the heavenly Jerusalem, so gloriously envisioned in the apocalypse of John, are those whose names are inscribed in the book of the Lamb.

The signing or inscribing of one's name in the Rite of Election is a weighty gesture. One has only to look at the Vietnam War Memorial in Washington, D.C., and view the reactions of people who come to see it to be impressed and even awed by the symbolic power of the names. The names in the Book of the Elect are names of the living, not the dead, but they too have power. And the act of writing them in the book has power. Written in the Book of the Elect—that book of the church that points to the sacrament of regeneration and therefore to eternal life—the names and all they represent are thus brought together in symbolic fashion with all who have pledged their future to Christ through the ages. The fact that many of these have never signed a ceremonial book—apostles, martyrs, saints, and, for that matter, the baptized candidates—makes no difference. They have put their names on the line by the way they have lived their lives. Repeated, simple, appropriate use of the ritual of enrollment makes the names, the book and the signing one powerful whole. Confused, changeable and complicated treatment of this part of the rite can only dissipate its power.

Chapter 7

When Did You Feel Chosen?

■

A standard opening gambit for catechetical sessions in the catechumenate is to appeal to the experience of those being catechized. In fact, much of the method currently in vogue in the catechumenate for adults relies heavily on what might be called the experiential basis of knowledge and action. As in the "shared Christian praxis"[1] method, which is widely influential in catechumenate catechesis, the first step is to identify what experience one has of the topic at hand. Succeeding steps in this process explore various dimensions of that experience, present the Christian tradition (i.e., what Christians have done in relation to this topic), place the participants' experience in dialogue with the tradition and, finally and consequently, arrive at a new way of doing things that represents a synthesis of the above. This method is generally very fruitful. Its aims are, beyond question, good ones, and its results are often admirable.

But when applying this kind of catechetical method to the subject of election, one must walk carefully. The simple question of "What has been your experience of divine election?" or, in more popular language, "When did you feel chosen?"—that is, when did you come to that inner certainty or knowledge of being among the elect of God—may be a fine starting place for the spiritual heirs of Calvinism, who believe that you can know that you are elect. But it is a terrible starting place for Catholics, who are forbidden by their own doctrine on the subject to claim this kind of knowledge apart from a special revelation from God.[2] The problem here is not only that election is a great mystery of our religion, like the Trinity or the hypostatic union, which does not easily admit of being grounded in experience because we know of it primarily through revelation. The problem is also a pastoral one: If we encourage people to look for assurance of their election in their own experience, the results will to some extent have to be falsified in order to achieve the desired effect. We do not *know* that we are the elect. That is simply a fact. Thus, the appropriate Catholic answer to the challenge of the evangelical preacher's question "Are you saved?" (which is just another way of asking if you are elect), quite seriously, is not "yes" but "I hope so."

One of the problems of the late medieval church to which the theology of the Protestant Reformation responded was widespread anxiety about attaining salvation. The fear of hell (which was expected to be the fate of most people) and the uncertainty of ever being able to reach the blessedness of God's kingdom were so strong in Christendom at that time that the preaching of justification by faith alone and the notion that God communicates to the believer a sure knowledge of his or her own election appeared to many as a liberation. Today the certainties of subjectivist religion are still experienced as a liberation, though this time not from the church but from the terrors of modern life. People search within themselves not so much for the sure hope that they will not go to hell but for assurance that they are not in hell already—that is, that they are not living a meaningless and powerless life.

The rhetoric of evangelical Protestantism in America is full of language about adult conversion that relies on subjective certainties that are, in some ways, very appealing, but against which Catholics must hold some reservations. Election is a case in point. It is easy to absorb some of the dominant Protestant culture's reflexes about this doctrine without realizing it. Catholics who think they know that they are elect because of some conversion experiences they have had are showing symptoms of having picked up a little crypto-Calvinism from their friends and neighbors.

In late twentieth-century Roman Catholicism we are also engaged in a kind of dialectic of reform. Many Catholics regard Catholicism as changing from a religion dominated by morbid concern over personal sinfulness to a religion infused with personal experience of the love of God, and from a religion that favors institutions to a religion that favors people. This is, in fact, a caricature both of the failings of the old and the achievements of the new. But it is nonetheless true that many people conceive of what is positive in the development of post–Vatican II Catholicism in just this way. The reform-oriented element in the church is, in fact, very devoted to promoting con- sciousness of the positive aspects of personal experience, reflection on personal history as mediating the divine, development of sovereign individual conscience, and the cultivation of personal experience of the love of God—in short, devoted to building up the individual subject with various assurances and reassurances.

In such a context, it is perhaps inevitable that the idea of being chosen by God suggests that the benefit to be gained by knowing, understanding and embracing the doctrine of election is an increased sense of being affirmed as a person. The aim of the exercise of "getting in touch with" experiences of divine election is ultimately to have the catechumen arrive at a stronger religious conviction of personal worthiness.[3] "I hope so" does not sound like a very satisfactory answer in the face of the ego needs that people bring with them to the project of Christian initiation. If we cannot know personally that we are elect, how can we find anything at all for us in this doctrine?

When we start at the wrong end of the equation, election indeed seems like a riddle. But election is not a riddle; the problem is that we are starting at the wrong end of the question. Thomas Aquinas locates his discussion of election and predestination within his discussion of divine providence, which is not soteriology but is part of the doctrine of God. Likewise, Augustine's discussion of election, which hammers away at human pretensions of having gained any of God's grace by their own merits, forces the issue always back to who God is and what God does. Karl Barth, whose theology of election is radically christological, totally rejects experience as a starting place and insists that the key must be sought in what we know by means of God's revelation in Christ.

If we begin our catechetical approach to the question of election from the side of theology rather than from the side of human experience, we get a whole different view of what is going on. We see history and the life of faith itself oriented toward a goal; we see the gift of Christ to the world as a triumph over the reign of sin; we see the divine life, in which we are called to participate, as mercy within mercy within mercy. Then, when we come to the question, "Am I a part of this?" "Is this indeed mine?" "Am I one of the elect?" the person who answers "This is my hope" has made a tremendous answer—indeed, the best of all possible answers. Because if this is your hope, if you do hope so, like an arrow shot at a target[4] the rest of your life will fly in that direction, toward that end, toward that last thing that baptism and all of the Christian life is about.

As John Berntsen has pointed out,[5] an important goal of catechumenate catechesis, modeled on the Fathers of the patristic period, is the development of Christian affections — that is to say, emotions integral to the substance of the teachings that are being embraced. To hope with a better hope and love with a better love — because the object of that hope and that love is a better object than that which you hoped for and loved in the past — is not only a legitimate but a necessary aspect of Christian conversion. Catechesis about election is a good example of this kind of integrated affective/intellectual/practical development. The benefit to be gained by knowing, understanding and embracing the doctrine of election is the development of the theological virtue of hope[6] and, consequently, the development of a greater capacity to act according to that hope. The catechumens may never have felt chosen by God in their lives. It hardly matters. What matters is that they have placed their hope in the God of Jesus Christ and have been trying to act accordingly.

Conclusion

■

The Rite of Election is about election. It is not about the bishop, the cathedral, how we feel about ourselves, or any of the great things we have done. It is about God out working out his purposes in our midst, in the catechumens and candidates, for the life of the world. In it—as in all the initiation rites—the church, that "elect lady," is bringing children of the promise to birth, each of them with a name, a hope and a destiny in God because of what Christ has done.

What does it look like? Although it varies from place to place, I can offer at least one strong example from a recent celebration in New York—not a model but a sample of something that people found to be effective. St. Patrick's Cathedral is a Gothic-style cathedral with a center aisle 150 feet long and 8 feet wide, and pews that seat about 2,000 people. We prepared for the rite carefully beforehand, rehearsing with representatives from the parishes, the hospitality volunteers and the liturgical ministers.

When people arrived at the cathedral on the afternoon of the First Sunday of Lent, they took part in a bilingual liturgy of the word that used the readings of that Sunday. The archbishop preached on the readings and emphasized mission. Though the diocesan coordinator presented the catechumens, when they were invited forward by the archbishop, it was the parish representative (usually the catechumenate director) who announced the name and location of the parish from a microphone in the center aisle. As each parish group was identified, those catechumens and their godparents came forward. They stood in a semicircle in the sanctuary, leaving an opening for the center aisle. Five hundred seventy-six people had come forward by the time all the parishes were announced. Then, from the center of this semicircle, the archbishop addressed them, asking first the godparents for their testimony, which they delivered in a loud voice, and then the catechumens for their assent. He then invited them to offer their names for enrollment.

Representatives of the 66 parishes present at that celebration were waiting in single file halfway down the center aisle, holding the books of the elect that had been signed earlier during the parish Rite of Sending. At the archbishop's invitation, they lifted up the books, held them high and made a stately procession down the aisle through the catechumens and into the sanctuary as the assembly sang "Here I am, Lord; I come to do your will." Each book was brought before the archbishop, held at chest height, open. He made a sign of the cross over the names in each book, and then the representatives proceeded to assemble in the sanctuary in another great semicircle (two deep), facing the catechumens and godparents, with the archbishop now in the center of the completed circle. As he announced the act of election, the representatives raised the books again, in a triumphant gesture, then brought them down and closed them. The elect were then warmly entrusted to the care of their godparents, who embraced them and returned with them to their seats. Through this ritual, the enthusiasm of the assembly had built so much that applause broke out spontaneously at every sung refrain as the elect returned to their places.

The ritual for the candidates followed the same pattern, though without the procession with books. Yet it had its own distinctive character. Because the candidates were so numerous (560, each with a sponsor; 1,120 people in all), they formed the shape of a cross as they assembled across the front of the sanctuary and down the center aisle. Unlike the catechumens, who came from all sides, we had arranged that the candidates should all come from one direction, down the middle aisle. The visual effect was comparable to that of a Cecil B. DeMille production—great movements of people, a cast of thousands, the Exodus revisited. The testimony of their sponsors rang out even more loudly, and as they returned to their places to the refrain of "Pueblo Libre," the assembly again broke into cheers.

We prayed, the elect and candidates were blessed, and we were dismissed; at least some of the people reported that they went home singing. Those who wanted to shake the archbishop's hand stayed and did so. The 4:00 PM Mass got a late start, but the rector said "For this . . . ?" and brushed our apologies aside. People who were waiting in the narthex for the 4:00 Mass were heard to murmur "Who are these people?" Who indeed? The elect, every one of them, some of them expecting to be baptized at Easter.

Endnotes

Introduction

[1] *Rite of Christian Initiation of Adults,* #119. The church's action is called "election," in quotation marks, to show that the word is used metaphorically when it refers to human action. The second part of paragraph 119 goes on to say that "the acceptance made by the church is founded on the election [no quotation marks] by God, in whose name the church acts."

[2] See the *Rite of Christian Initiation of Adults: Provisional Text* (Washington DC: USCC Office of Publishing Services, 1974), #23. This phrase was unfortunately left out of the 1988 version for use in the dioceses of the United States, in which some of the introductory material was reworked, though it remains in the *editio typica* (foundational Latin text). The omission in the 1988 American version seems to have been made for stylistic reasons: the expression "focal point" is used shortly afterwards in the new redaction (RCIA [1988], #121; compare with RCIA [1974], #135). Of course, "focal point" is the weaker expression. The word *cardinem* can also be translated as hinge or pivot: *"Quapropter patet electionem, quae tanta sollemnitate ornatur, veluti cardinem esse totius catechumenatus"* (Ordo Initiationis Christianae Adultorum [Vatican City, Polyglot Press, 1972]), #23.

[3] This is a shorthand way of referring to any of several forms of the parish rite that sends people to the diocesan rite.

[4] Sending of the Catechumens for Election (#106ff.); Election or Enrollment of Names (#118ff.); Rite of Election or Enrollment of Names (of children who have reached catechetical age) (#277ff.); Rite of Sending the Candidates for Recognition by the Bishop and for the Call to Continuing Conversion (#434ff.); Rite of Calling the Candidates to Continuing Conversion (#446ff.); Parish Celebration for Sending Catechumens for Election and Candidates for Recognition by the Bishop (#530ff.); Celebration of the Rite of Election of Catechumens and the Call to Continuing Conversion of Candidates Who Are Preparing for Confirmation and/or Eucharist or Reception into the Full Communion of the Catholic Church (#562ff.).

Chapter 1

[1] *Relatio* of *Schemata,* n. 112, *De Rituali* 5, 4 October 1965 (ICEL archives, Washington, D.C.), part II, #2–5, of the *Praemittenda:* "De principiis generalibus instaurationis."

95

Note also that precedence is always given to the Roman tradition.

[2]See Vatican Council II, *Constitution on the Sacred Liturgy (Sacrosanctum Concilium), #64–66; Decree on the Church's Missionary Activity (Ad Gentes), #14; Decree on the Pastoral Office of Bishops (Christus Dominus),* #14.

[3]RCIA, #124. Unless otherwise noted, the abbreviation RCIA will always refer to the 1988 text and follow its numbering system.

[4]*Relatio* of *Schemata* n. 112, #3.

[5]Michel Dujarier argues that the pattern of two thresholds for baptism— the latter of which corresponds to Election—can be seen in the narratives of the baptisms of Pentecost, and the baptism of Cornelius particularly, in the Acts of the Apostles. Michel Dujarier, *A History of the Catechumenate,* trans. Edward J. Haasl, ed. Kevin Hart (New York: William H. Sadlier, Inc., 1979), 19–21.

[6]The fact that there were two stages is significant. The catechumenate was not simply one continuous sweep from the time a catechumen entered it until the sacraments were celebrated. Those who were to receive the sacraments had to be "chosen" after the process of initiation was well underway, and only then could they approach its consummation in the sacraments.

[7]This is attested to by St. Cyril and Egeria concerning the church in Jerusalem, by Pope Siricius for the church in Rome, by the Fourth Council of Carthage and St. Augustine for the church in North Africa, and by St. Augustine for the church in Milan. See G. Bareille, "Catéchuménat," *Dictionnaire de theologie catholique,* vol. 2 (Paris: Letouzey et Ané, Editeurs, 1910), col. 1976.

[8]St. Cyril and Egeria, the Canons of Hippolytus, Ambrose, etc.

[9]The fourth Council of Carthage prescribes that "Those who are to be baptized give their names" (Canon 85). St. Basil of Caesarea, St. Gregory of Nyssa, St. Ambrose of Milan and St. Augustine of Hippo all make reference to the giving of names in preparation for baptism. See both P. de Puniet, "Catéchuménat," *Dictionnaire d'archéologie chrétienne et Liturgie* (Paris: Letouzey et Ané, Editeurs, 1907), col. 2591, and Bareille, col. 1976.

[10]Bareille, col. 1976.

[11]Gregory Dix, ed., *The Treatise on the Apostolic Tradition of St. Hippolytus of Rome,* vol. 1 (London: S.P.C.K., 1937), XXXIV–XXXV.

[12]Unless otherwise noted, all quotations from the *Apostolic Tradition* are from Dix's translation (see note 11). For the convenience of the reader, I have followed each quotation with the abbreviation AT and Dix's chapter and verse numbers, even when I have preferred to use a different translation.

[13]Geoffrey J. Cuming, *Hippolytus: A Text for Students* (Bramcote: Grove Books, 1976), 17.

[14]*Egeria's Travels to the Holy Land,* revised ed., trans. John Wilkinson (Jerusalem: Ariel Publishing

House, 1981), 143. (Unless otherwise noted, the translation is taken from Wilkinson. For the reader's convenience, I have supplied Wilkinson's chapter and verse numbers in the text, following the abbreviation E, even when I use another translation.)

¹⁵Leonel L. Mitchell, *Worship: Initiation and the Churches* (Washington DC: Pastoral Press, 1991), 25.

¹⁶E. C. Whitaker, *Documents of the Baptismal Liturgy* (London: S.P.C.K., 1970), 42. This translation is taken from *The Pilgrimage of Etheria,* eds. M.L. McClure and C.L. Feltoe (S.P.C.K., 1919).

¹⁷Whitaker, 45.

¹⁸Whitaker, 38. This phrase is taken from the Stavronikita Series, No. 2, paragraph 9.

¹⁹Theodore of Mopsuestia recalls that a "duly appointed person" wrote down the names, both of the elect and the godparent (Whitaker, 45.) Although we do not know who this "duly appointed person" might have been, it is unlikely that he would have been the bishop.

²⁰Whitaker, 44. See also Wilkinson (E 46.4): "At ordinary services when the bishop sits and preaches, ladies and sisters, the faithful utter exclamations, but when they come and hear him explaining the catechesis, their exclamations are far louder, God is my witness."

²¹RCIA, #122.

²²The one option that is *not* offered is that the bishop write the names

himself. Thus we part company with fifth-century Jerusalem, which seems to have been idiosyncratic in that regard anyway.

²³Whitaker, 45.

²⁴RCIA, #123.

Chapter 2

¹B[althasar] Fischer, "De Initiatione christiana adultorum" *Notitiae* 3 (1967): 65.

²The first intercession, inspired by Pope Celestine (*Migne*, PL 50, 535), asks that when the elect are "led to the sacraments of rebirth," the Lord will "deign to unbolt the inner court of the mercies of heaven" for them (my translation). The next two intercessions, based on writings of St. John Chrysostom, pray for protection against the snares of the devil and the temptations of the world, and that the elect may be confirmed and always preserved in their faith. The last three concern the church, the Holy Spirit and illumination in truth. (From *Schemata,* n. 147, *De Rituali* 9, 18 March 1966 [ICEL archives, Washington, D.C.], #46, p. 23–24.)

³What was envisioned was a kind of calling of the community to undertake their responsibilities to the elect in the period leading to Easter. "To assure the participation of the community in the rite of election, one does not seek to diversify the 'ideological' themes of the different intentions but to underline the liturgical movement which leads the entire community toward Easter,

and the responsibility of this community in regard to the catechumens" (my translation). See notes from the *Session du Coetus XXII,* Vanves, France; December 30, 1968–January 4, 1969 (ICEL archives, Washington, D.C.), 16.

⁴The 1974 English translation rendered *gratia* in this prayer as "love" rather than grace—a move that should (and apparently did) leave us gasping. It was retranslated correctly as "grace" in the 1988 version.

⁵For instance, the word "enrollment" made people confuse this rite with the one held at the beginning of the catechumenate. Those who held a discernment before the rite felt that the rite was merely a restatement of facts already established. Vanves, *passim.*

⁶Vanves, 14.

⁷Vanves, 15.

⁸Balthasar Fischer, chairman of the *coetus* that produced the RCIA, was asked in an interview in 1983 why the Rite of Election had been omitted in chapter 5, for children of catechetical age. He said he did not remember the reason, that possibly it was to simplify things for the children ("Interview with Balthasar Fischer," *The Chicago Catechumenate* 6 no. 2 (December 1983): 8. This vague reply, prefaced by his own disclaimer that he did not remember the reason, is quite inconclusive.

⁹For the origins of this rite and a discussion of its particulars, see Ronald A. Oakham, "Sending of the Catechumens for Election," in

Celebrating the Rites of Adult Initiation: Pastoral Reflections, ed. Victoria M. Tufano (Chicago: Liturgy Training Publications, 1992), 49–62.

¹⁰Michel Dujarier, *A History of the Catechumenate,* trans. Edward J. Haasl, ed. Kevin Hart (New York: William H. Sadlier, 1979), 85ff.

Chapter 3

¹Jacques Guillet, "Election," trans. Glicerio S. Abad, in *Dictionary of Biblical Theology,* 2nd edition, ed. Xavier Léon-Dufour (New York: The Seabury Press, 1973), 137.

²Walther Eichrodt, *Theology of the Old Testament,* Vol. 1, tr. by J. A. Baker (Philadelphia: The Westminster Press, 1961), 43.

³Guillet, 140–1.

⁴G. C. Berkouwer, *Divine Election,* trans. Hugo Bekker (Grand Rapids: Wm. B. Eerdmans Publishing Co., 1960), 51.

⁵"On the Predestination of the Saints," and "On the Gift of Perseverance," in *Saint Augustine: Anti-Pelagian Writings,* Vol. 5 of *A Select Library of Nicene and Post-Nicene Fathers of the Christian Church,* ed. by Philip Schaff (Grand Rapids: Wm. B. Eerdmans Publishing Co., 1956), 497–552.

⁶For a résumé of numerous discussions bearing on election within the theological circle of the Reformed churches, see Berkouwer, *op. cit.*

⁷Karl Barth's extensive treatment of election (*Church Dogmatics,* Vol. 2,

Book 2), in many respects a creative departure from classical reformed doctrines, has drawn comment from Catholic theologians, notably Jerome Hamer, OP *(Karl Barth)*, and Hans Urs von Balthasar, SJ *(The Theology of Karl Barth)*. Their own constructive contributions to the discussion are limited, but it is worth noting that although they disagree with some of Barth's particular points within his more than 600-page discussion of election, neither of them challenge his fundamental thesis. Joseph Cardinal Ratzinger even appeals to it in his work *The Meaning of Christian Brotherhood.* Nevertheless, the fact remains that there are no Catholic theologians of the twentieth century whose writings on election might compare with Karl Barth's or even with Wolfart Pannenberg's brief but stimulating treatment of election as the key to developing a theology of history *(Human Nature, Election and History)*. Karl Rahner's discussion of the doctrine of God in the New Testament *(Theological Investigations,* Vol. 1) is pregnant with the theme of election but never quite delivers.

[8] Allan Bouley, "Election or Enrollment of Names," in *Commentaries: Rite of Christian Initiation of Adults,* ed. James A. Wilde (Chicago: Liturgy Training Publications, 1988), 25.

[9] "The chosen people" or "God's people" is synonymous with "the elect" or "the elect of God."

[10] John Bright, *A History of Israel,* 2nd edition (Philadelphia: The Westminster Press, 1972), 144.

[11] The call of Abraham is the reading assigned for the Rite of Acceptance into the Order of Catechumens; the Exodus account of Israel's escape through the Red Sea is the central Old Testament text of the Easter Vigil.

[12] Gerhard von Rad's treatment of the theological shape of the "primal history"—that set of stories at the beginning of the book of Genesis which immediately precede the call of Abraham and hence the beginning of the "saving history," that is, the story of God's relationship to Israel—helps to shed light on how Israel understood its election in relation to the nations. See Gerhard von Rad, *Old Testament Theology,* Vol. 1, trans. D. M. G. Stalker (New York: Harper & Row Publishers, 1962), 161–165.

[13] Walther Zimmerli, *Old Testament Theology in Outline,* trans. David E. Green (Atlanta: John Knox Press, 1978), 169.

[14] Zimmerli, 173; also von Rad, 156–157.

[15] von Rad, 163.

[16] Yehezkel Kaufmann, *The Religion of Israel: From Its Beginnings to the Babylonian Exile,* trans. and abr. Moshe Greenberg (Chicago: University of Chicago Press, 1960), 299.

[17] Harold H. Rowley, *The Biblical Doctrine of Election* (London: Lutterworth Press, 1950), 45ff. Rowley also makes the point that election outside the covenant (e.g., as Isaiah regarded Assyria, or Jeremiah and Habakkuk saw the Chaldaeans, or Deutero-Isaiah described Cyrus of

ENDNOTES

Persia) is election to service too: see 121–138.

[18]Karl Barth, *Church Dogmatics,* vol. 2, trans. G. W. Bromily et. al. (New York: Charles Scribner's Sons, 1957), 30–31.

[19]Karl Barth's frequent use of the term "affirmation" in his theological reflections on election denotes more than a psychological meaning.

[20]Rowley, 147–49.

[21]Alan Richardson, *An Introduction to the Theology of the New Testament* (New York: Harper and Row Publishers, 1958), 267.

[22]David M. Stanley and Raymond E. Brown, "Aspects of New Testament Thought," in *The Jerome Biblical Commentary,* ed. Raymond E. Brown, Joseph A. Fitzmyer, and Roland Murphy (Englewood Cliffs, NJ: Prentice-Hall, Inc., 1968) 78:72, p. 779.

[23]Richardson 277–78. Cf. Enoch 39:6; 40:5; 45:3f.; 49:2, 4; 51:3, 5; 52:6, 9; 55:4; 61:4f., 8, 10.

[24]The messianic community is sometimes imagined as a woman bearing children. See P. S. Minear, "Elect Lady," in *The Interpreter's Dictionary of the Bible,* vol. 2, ed. George Arthur Buttrick (New York: Abingdon Press, 1962), 76.

[25]The reading *ho eklektos tou theou* appears in P5, Codex Sinaiticus, particular MSS of some of the versions (Itala and Syriac), and in Ambrose. The reading *ho eklektos huios tou theou* is found in some other MSS of the Itala and the Syriac, and in the Sahidic. (*The Greek New Testament,* 3rd ed. [corrected], ed. Kurt Aland, et al. [n.p.: United Bible Societies, 1983.]) Joseph Fitzmyer points out that this version is preferred by some translators (New English Bible, La Bible de Jérusalem) and scholars (A. Loisy, A. von Harnack, R. Schnackenburg, R. E. Brown) over that of better manuscripts (which read Son of God: *ho huios tou theou*) because it is thought to be more in keeping with older traditions concerning the baptism of Jesus, and because it is more likely that "elect" would be changed to "Son" rather than the other way around. (Joseph Fitzmyer, *Essays on the Semitic Background of the New Testament* [London: Geoffrey Chapman, 1971], 129.) *The New American Bible* (1970) also uses "elect of God."

[26]"This *krisis* aspect of Jesus' earthly career is seen to operate in John's conception of it as a courtroom drama, which begins with the deposition of the Baptist (1:19 ff.) and culminates, after a series of testimonies and accusations by 'the Jews,' in the 'judgment of this world' (12:31) wherein Jesus' self-appointed judges are themselves condemned. The legal terminology (judge, judgment, witness, testimony, accuse, convict, advocate, etc.) serves to underscore the fundamental Johannine conception of Jesus' work as *krisis.*" Stanley and Brown, 78:90, p. 782.

[27]The appearance of Moses and Elijah, the dazzling garments, the cloud and the voice from heaven all evoke Christ's glorious destiny.

Meanwhile, the conversation he is having with Moses and Elijah is about his death, and passages immediately preceding this talk about taking up one's cross (vv. 23–24). A second prediction of Christ's passion follows soon after the transfiguration (v. 44).

28 There, the "leaders of the people," who are watching Jesus die, say, "He saved others, let him save himself if he is the Messiah of God, the chosen one *(eklektos)*." The irony of the scoffers' taunt lies in the fact that precisely because he is the elect of God, Jesus has given himself over to the suffering of the cross.

29 Paul, though he struggles with the painful circumstances of the partial rejection of Jesus by the Jewish people, continues to believe that God's faithfulness to their election is enduring and to hope for an eventual reconciliation (though he abandons hope that Israel will be converted first, before the Gentiles).

30 This quotation from Isaiah is from the Septuagint.

31 See also Romans 9:33, and 1 Corinthians 1:23.

32 H. Preisker, F. L. Cross, R. Perdelwitz, and M. E. Boismard. F. L. Cross argues that most of the letter is taken from the presider's part in the baptismal liturgy of Hippolytus. For a summary of arguments concerning the so-called "liturgical hypothesis," see J. N. D. Kelly, *A Commentary on the Epistles of Peter and Jude* (New York: Harper and Row Publishers, 1969), 16ff., and Francis Wright Beare, *The First Epistle of Peter*, 2nd ed., revised

(Oxford: Blackwell & Mott Ltd., 1958), 196–202.

33 For a summary of sources that support this position, see John S. Mbiti, *New Testament Eschatology in an African Background* (London: Oxford University Press, 1971), 98–101.

34 The only human action indicated by the terminology of the ancient rite is "petitioning" (as in *competentes*), in which case the subject is the catechumen.

Chapter 5

1 In fact, the bishop does not ordinarily reconvene with all the elect of the diocese for the Scrutinies, so this is usually left out in practice.

Chapter 6

1 "As a pledge of fidelity the candidates inscribe their names," RCIA, #119.

2 See Thomas Aquinas, *Summa Theologiae* (n.p.: Blackfriars, 1967) vol 5, *God's Will and Providence,* 1a 24, 3:3.

3 Cf. Revelation 3:5; 13:8; 17:8; 20:15; 21:27; 20:12; Hebrews 12:33.

4 Cf. Exodus 32:32, 33; Psalm 69:28; Psalm 139:16.

5 Augustine, *City of God* XX.14, cf. Revelation 20:12.

6 Cf. Sirach 24:23 (v. 32 in the Vulgate).

ENDNOTES

7 *Summa* 1a.24,1:1. Aquinas does not hold that evil deeds are recorded in the book, however.

8Berkouwer, 110.

9See also the Formula of Concord.

10*Institutes* III, XXVI, 5.

objectives of that period: "the catechumens learn . . . in all things to keep their hopes set on Christ" (RCIA, #75.2).

Chapter 7

1Thomas Groome, *Christian Religious Education* (San Francisco: Harper & Row), 1980.

2Denzinger, *Enchiridion Symbolorum,* #805 and #825 (refers to the Council of Trent); see also #806 and #826 with regard to the related matter of the gift of perseverance.

3It might be argued that the logical term of coming into a knowledge of God's election would result rather in a profound sense of *unworthiness,* and thus produce both a font of gratitude and a passion to "make a return to the Lord for all the good he has done for me" (Psalm 116:12).

4Thomas Aquinas uses the metaphor of the arrow, with God as the archer, to illustrate predestination (*Summa* 1a 23,1).

5John A. Berntsen, "Christian Affections and the Catechumenate," *Worship* 52 (1978): 194–210.

6It is interesting to note that the *praenotanda* for the catechumenate period make specific mention of the reorientation of hope as one of the

Select Bibliography

Augustine. *The City of God*. Translated by Marcus Dods. In *Augustine*, vol. 18 of *Great Books of the Western World*, edited by Robert Maynard Hutchins. Chicago: William Benton, 1952.

_____. "On the Gift of Perseverance," "On Grace and Free Will," and "On the Predestination of the Saints." Translated by Peter Holmes and Robert Ernest Wallis. In *A Select Library of Nicene and Post-Nicene Fathers of the Christian Church*. Vol. 5, *Saint Augustine: Anti-Pelagian Writings*. Edited by Philip Schaff. Grand Rapids: Wm. B. Eerdmans Publishing Co., 1956.

Balthasar, Hans Urs von. *The Theology of Karl Barth*. Translated by John Drury. New York: Holt, Rinehart and Winston, 1971.

Bareille, G. "Catéchuménat." In *Dictionaire de theologie catholique*, vol. 2. Paris: Letouzey et Ané, Editeurs, 1910, col. 1968–1987.

Barth, Karl. *Church Dogmatics*. Vol. 2, *The Doctrine of God*. Translated by G. W. Bromily, et al. New York: Charles Scribner's Sons, 1957.

Battenhouse, Roy W., ed. *A Companion to the Study of St. Augustine*. New York: Oxford University Press, 1955.

Beare, Francis Wright. *The First Epistle of Peter*, 2nd edition, revised. Oxford: Blackwell & Mott Ltd., 1958.

Berkouwer, G. C. *Divine Election*. Translated by Hugo Bekker. Grand Rapids: Wm. B. Eerdmans Publishing Co., 1960.

Berntsen, John A. "Christian Affections and the Catechumenate." *Worship* 52 (1978): 194–210.

Bouley, Allan. "Election or Enrollment of Names." In *Commentaries: Rite of Christian Initiation of Adults,* edited by James A. Wilde. Chicago: Liturgy Training Publications, 1988.

Bright, John. *A History of Israel.* 2nd Edition. Philadelphia: The Westminster Press, 1972.

Calvin, Jean. *Institutes of the Christian Religion.* Translated by Ford Lewis Battles. In *Library of Christian Classics.* Vols. 20 and 21, *Calvin: Institutes of the Christian Religion.* Edited by John T. McNeill. Philadelphia: The Westminster Press, 1960.

Chadwick, Henry. *The Early Church.* Harmondsworth: Penguin Books Ltd., 1967.

Cuming, Geoffrey J. *Hippolytus: A Text for Students.* Grove Liturgical Study No. 8. Bramcote: Grove Books, 1976.

Denzinger, Henricus. *Enchiridion Symbolorum: Definitionum et Declarationum de Rebus Fidei et Morum.* Friburgi-Brisgoviae: Herder & Co., 1937.

Dix, Gregory, editor. *The Treatise on the Apostolic Tradition of St. Hippolytus of Rome,* vol. 1. London: S.P.C.K., 1937.

Dujarier, Michel. *A History of the Catechumenate.* Translated by Edward J. Haasl and edited by Kevin Hart. New York: William H. Sadlier, 1979.

_____. *The Rites of Christian Initiation: Historical and Pastoral Reflections.* Translated and edited by Kevin Hart. New York: William H. Sadlier, Inc., 1979.

Eichrodt, Walther. *Theology of the Old Testment,* vol. 1. Translated by J. A. Baker. Philadelphia: The Westminster Press, 1961.

Fischer, B[althasar]. "De Initiatione christiana adultorum." *Notitiae* 3 (1967): 55–70.

Fitzmyer, Joseph A. *Essays on the Semitic Background of the New Testament.* London: Goeffrey Chapman, 1971.

Groome, Thomas. *Christian Religious Education.* San Francisco: Harper & Row, 1980.

Guillet, Jacques. "Election." Translated by Glicerio S. Abad. In *Dictionary of Biblical Theology.* 2d ed. Edited by Xavier Léon-Dufour. New York: The Seabury Press, 1973.

Hamer, Jerome. *Karl Barth.* Translated by Dominic M. Maruca. Westminster MD: The Newman Press, 1962.

"An Interview with Balthasar Fischer." *The Chicago Catechumenate* 6, no. 2 (December 1983): 7–14.

Kaufmann, Yehezkel. *The Religion of Israel: From Its Beginnings to the Babylonian Exile.* Translated and abridged by Moshe Greenberg. Chicago: University of Chicago Press, 1960.

Kelly, J. N. D. *A Commentary on the Epistles of Peter and Jude.* New York: Harper and Row, Publishers, 1969.

Laurentin, André, and Michel Dujarier. *Catéchuménat: Données de l'histoire et perspectives nouvelles.* Paris: Éditions du Centurion, 1969.

Loveley, E. "Election, Divine." In *New Catholic Encyclopedia.* New York: McGraw-Hill Book Co., 1969.

Maertens, Th[iery]. *Histoire et pastorale du rituel du catéchuménat et du baptême.* Bruges: Publications de Saint-André, 1962.

Mbiti, John S. *New Testament Eschatology in an African Background.* London: Oxford University Press, 1971.

Mendenhall, G. E. "Election." In *The Interpreter's Dictionary of the Bible,* edited by George Arthur Buttrick. New York: Abingdon Press, 1962.

Minear, P[aul]. S. "Elect Lady." In *The Interpreter's Dictionary of the Bible,* edited by George Arthur Buttrick. New York: Abingdon Press, 1962.

Mitchell, Leonel L. *Worship: Initiation and the Churches.* Washington, DC: Pastoral Press, 1991.

Molin, Jean-Baptiste. "Le Nouveau rituel de l'initiation chrétienne des adultes" *Notitiae* 8 (1972): 87–95.

Murphy Center for Liturgical Research. *Made, Not Born: New Perspectives on Christian Initiation and the Catechumenate.* Notre Dame: University of Notre Dame Press, 1976.

Nocent, Adrian. *The Liturgical Year.* Vol. 2, *Lent.* Translated by Matthew J. O'Connell. Collegeville: The Liturgical Press, 1977.

Oakham, Ronald A. "Sending of the Catechumens for Election." In *Celebrating the Rites of Adult Initiation: Pastoral Reflections,* edited by Victoria Tufano. Chicago: Liturgy Training Publications, 1992.

Ordo Initiationis Christianae Adultorum. Vatican City: Polyglot Press, 1972.

Palladino, A. G. "Predestination (in Catholic Theology)." In *New Catholic Encyclopedia.* New York: McGraw-Hill Book Co., 1967.

Pannenberg, Wolfhart. *Human Nature, Election and History.* Philadelphia: The Westminster Press, 1977.

Portalie, Eugene. *A Guide to the Thought of Saint Augustine.* Translated by Ralph J. Bastian. Chicago: Henry Regnery Company, 1960.

Puniet, P. de. "Catéchuménat." In *Dictionnaire d'archéologie chrétienne et de Liturgie.* Paris: Letouzey et Ané, Editeurs, 1907, col. 2579–2621.

Rahner, Karl. *Theological Investigations.* Vol. 1, *God, Christ, Mary and Grace.* Translated by Cornelius Ernst. Baltimore: Helicon Press, 1961.

Ratzinger, Joseph. *The Meaning of Christian Brotherhood.* 2d English edition. (First published as *Die christliche Brüderlichkeit.* Kösel-Ferlag, Munich, 1960) San Francisco: Ignatius Press, 1993.

Relatio for *Schemata* n. 112, *De Rituali* 5, October 4, 1965. ICEL archives, Washington DC.

Richardson, Alan. *An Introduction to the Theology of the New Testament.* New York: Harper & Row Publishers, 1958.

The Rite of Christian Initiation of Adults. Chicago: Liturgy Training Publications, 1988.

The Rite of Christian Initiation of Adults: Provisional Text. Washington DC: USCC Office of Publishing Services, 1974.

Rowley, Harold H. *The Biblical Doctrine of Election.* London: Lutterworth Press, 1950.

Schemata, n. 147, *De Rituali* 9, March 18, 1966. ICEL archives, Washington DC.

Scott, R. B. Y. *The Relevance of the Prophets.* rev. ed. New York: Macmillan Publishing Co., Inc., 1968.

Session du Coetus XXII (Vanves, France), December 30, 1968– January 4, 1969. [Both this document and its English translation bear the date October 30, 1968–January 4, 1969. But this appears to be an error. The *Relatio* of the *Schemata,* n. 352, *De Rituali,* n. 36 states in paragraph #13 that the meeting in question began on December 30, and I have adopted this date as the more plausible one.] ICEL archives, Washington DC.

Sharp, Douglas R. *The Hermeneutics of Election: The Significance of the Doctrine in Barth's Church Dogmatics.* Lanham: University Press of America, Inc., 1990.

Stanley, David M., and Raymond E. Brown. "Aspects of New Testament Thought." In *The Jerome Biblical Commentary,* edited by Raymond E. Brown, Joseph A. Fitzmyer and Roland E. Murphy. Englewood Cliffs, NJ: Prentice-Hall, Inc., 1968.

Talley, Thomas J. *The Origins of the Liturgical Year.* New York: Pueblo Publishing Co., 1986.

Thomas Aquinas. *Summa Theologiae*. Vol. 5, *God's Will and Providence* (1a. 19–26). Translated by Thomas Gilby. n.p.: Blackfriars, 1967.

von Rad, Gerhard. *Old Testament Theology*, vol. 1. Translated by D. M. G. Stalker. New York: Harper & Row Publishers, 1962.

Whitaker, E. C. *Documents of the Baptismal Liturgy*. London: S.P.C.K., 1970.

Wilkinson, John. *Egeria's Travels to the Holy Land*. rev. ed. Jerusalem: Ariel Publishing House, 1981.

Willis, Geoffrey Grimshaw. *St. Augustine's Lectionary*. London: S.P.C.K., 1962.

Yarnold, Edward. *The Awe-Inspiring Rites of Initiation: Baptismal Homilies of the Fourth Century*. Slough: St. Paul Publications, 1971.

Zimmerli, Walther. *Old Testament Theology in Outline*. Translated by David E. Green. Atlanta: John Knox Press, 1978.